HENRY JAMES

and the

EXPANDING HORIZON

A Study Of The Meaning And
Basic Themes of James's
Fiction

By

Osborn Andreas

GREENWOOD PRESS, PUBLISHERS
NEW YORK

To

MARIAN BARD

FOREWORD

One fine summer day some twenty-five years ago, a professor and two of his students were cruising together on the waters of Puget Sound. What port of call lay ahead of them I do not remember, nor do I recall what they talked about. A safe guess would include books, music, wine, women, and the state of the world. No untoward incident happened to mark out this day above many others of its kind, but the memory of pleasant, casual give and take of light-hearted minds has managed to survive competition with more pressing matters. In due time these two men dropped off the conveyor belt and rolled away to destinations unknown. Unlike the majority of students who pass by in yearly waves to disappear entirely from sight, these same two have again become entangled with my interests. One of them, George B. Vetter, now a professor of psychology in New York University, was a recent visitor to the campus for a summer session. From him I learned that the third member of my crew, Osborn Andreas, now a substantial man of affairs in the Middle West, had sent in to the University Press a manuscript bearing the title that proclaims this book, which he earnestly desired to have published by his old University. To undertake a revision of the manuscript and to engage the interest of the Press in its printing was a proposal that called for no argument. In the Irish idiom, "all it needed was the wind of a word." The happy result is the book now before us.

The courteous tribute which the author paid me in his Preface is of the kind that a teacher hugs to his heart, and it comes with a peculiar grace at a time when, after forty-five years of teaching, I am crossing the threshold of retirement.

To extend one's life into the future through intellectual stimulus is not too vain a desire; rather it is one of the chief consolations that relieve those painful moments of doubt that sometimes becloud the day for a professor. Pleasant as is the spoken word, the written statement lasts longer and carries farther. Perpetuity of memory rather than diuturnity of days still remains a major concern of a man who is not content merely to "subsist in bones," despite the mournful dictum of Sir Thomas Browne that such restless inquietude "seems a vanity almost out of date and superannuated piece of folly." So, far be it from me to reject an acknowledgment so freely offered.

The variegated career of Mr. Andreas is a counterbalance to the despairing view that once out of college a man keeps slipping back from the intellectual heights he had reached on graduation as he becomes absorbed in the business of earning a living. It is likewise an apt refutation of the attitude, happily now fading, that the man of affairs and the scholar belong to worlds whose intervening gap can never be bridged, an attitude expressed in Longfellow's "Morituri Salutamus" as well as anywhere:

> The scholar and the world! The endless strife,
> The discords in the harmonies of life!
> The love of learning, the sequestered nooks,
> And all the sweet serenity of books;
> The market place, the eager love of gain,
> Whose aim is vanity, and whose end is pain.

Longfellow lamented the changes he saw on revisiting Bowdoin College fifty years after his graduation. Had he lived till today, he would have seen the market place creeping up closer to the campus, insinuating itself into the curriculum, and even boldly taking its seat as a College of Economics and Business Administration. Other times, other manners!

In the present-day restoration of Henry James to his rightful claim as one of the major novelists in American literature, Mr. Andreas' book comes most opportunely, whether as an introduction for those who have never brought themselves to submit to James's wanderings of thought, or for those who already initiated wish to renew their delight in his exploration of this variable creature man. How Mr. Andreas came to be interested in a study of James may be read in his Preface. What he has not read about James has not yet been written. But it was the stories themselves, not the critics, that furnished the clue to the novelist's intentions, and the discovery, if such it were, that the key to a man's behavior was his conduct in the situations that activated it. In the mind of James, conduct was concerned with one's "awareness," or lack of it, in the use he made of his fellows. The burden of Mr. Andreas as critic was to center on establishing and elucidating this "awareness" as a unifying principle ever present in James's novels. To make good his thesis he has seen fit to disregard the multifarious interests and passions that make these novels so rich in implications. The consequent oversimplification both in criticism and in analysis of plot may tend to create a distorted conception of the novelist's power, especially for readers only slightly acquainted with James, unless they bear constantly in mind the writer's main concept of the "expanding horizon." But the critic's approach may be justified by the skill with which he has manipulated his material to isolate and accentuate his theory.

This work is far from pretending to be a study wherein

methodology, research, and documentation play their important roles. Rather it is the record of a highly sensitive and critical mind, which believes that it has found its way to some underlying drive compelling the novelist to shape in a given manner his experiences and reflections thereon as life has presented them to his consciousness.

Finally it remains to praise the subtle nuances of thought and the refreshing exactness of vocabulary that make the reading of this work so richly rewarding.

Edward G. Cox

University of Washington

PREFACE

Many of us who read fiction often find ourselves sufficiently puzzled by some story or novel to feel the need of exchanging ideas about it with a friend. Although we have read carefully enough to know exactly what happened, we may feel that "more is meant than meets the ear" and that we may be missing something that the story means to tell us. Conversation with friends often reveals, to our astonishment, violently differing accounts of the story's theme, subject, and meaning. We are then forced to conclude that there is no help for us except from those trained specialists, those expert readers, the literary critics.

The help which we expected to find in them, however, too often turns out to be as illusory as a mirage. We ask them for illumination of the story's content but are given either psychoanalytic, sociological, economic, moralistic treatises or irrelevant speculations (called "critical biographies") on the author's private life. Sometimes we will be favored with an analysis of the author's craftsmanship, of the stylistic and structural devices he uses to get his effects. Worthy as these discourses may be in their fields, they nevertheless leave us untutored with respect to the meaning of the story itself.

We have been taught that facts speak for themselves, but we often find ourselves wondering what the facts in a story are saying to us. It is not the business of the storyteller but our own to work out what is implied by the action of a story. If we, as readers, do not fathom the meaning which is implicated there, we waste the best part of a writer's work, since, missing the intention of the action, we are contenting ourselves with the mere incidental beauties of the performance.

Many of us are prone to substitute the moral or practical lesson which we think the story may teach for the meaning, thus confusing two distinct things. The moral is an abstraction, while the meaning is statable only in terms of the action which occurs within the story itself. Abstractions have a way of seeming more useful than they prove to be, whereas concrete and specific meanings, elusive as they are, light up not only the particular situation which contains them but also the multiplied instances supplied by our own experience.

As one reader to another, I wish to tell here of one thing I learned in writing this book. I found that the only effective way to discover the significance of a story was to retell it in my own words, that generalized comment without the retelling failed of its purpose. A condensed rehearsal of the action turned out, to my surprise, to furnish forth much more than a mere synopsis of the plot. It seems to be a psychological fact that, when one sets out to convey to a friend the contents of a story one has read, one's interpretation of the events gets inextricably mingled with the events themselves. In fact, one finds that one can define the meaning of an action only in terms of that action. To launch out into generalized comment without first having recited the concrete particular is to float free from the groundwork upon which the exegetical statement should rest.

The interpretative story summaries in the body of this book are, therefore, the proofs which demonstrate the truth of the statements made concerning James's basic insight, his single predominant meaning. They cannot in any degree substitute for the stories themselves; they merely enable us to get the lay of the land, to see the forest distantly as a unit instead of closely as many trees. The bird's-eye view which the summaries furnish should enable one, in rereading the text of the stories, to absorb more fully the significance of the details and to verify or refute the evidence which the summaries bring forward to support my account of the Jamesian sensibility.

My purpose in writing this book was equally to furnish the reader of Henry James's fiction with the kind of book that I remember feeling the need of when I first read James and to find out for myself what basic meaning, common to all his fiction, would become visible through comparing the themes of all his stories and novels, one with the other. These are not two purposes but two facets of one purpose— that of stating an impression against which other impressions can be checked. The interpretations I have advanced seem to me, of course, to be the correct ones, but their principal function would be, I should think, that of stimulating the reader to agreement and amplification or to disagreement and rebuttal, either of which would enhance his understanding of the stories and his pleasure in rereading them.

I wish here to acknowledge my debt to various persons without whom this book would have been either very differently written or probably not written at all. First, to Marian Bard, a personal friend, I owe a great deal for the exhaustive discussions which she and I have had about many of the James stories. Second, to Dr. George B. Vetter, Associate Professor of Psychology at New York University, I owe considerable in the way of general encouragement. Third, to Dr. Edward G. Cox, Professor of English at the

University of Washington, I owe a great debt. It was under his direction and due to his friendly criticism that I first learned to think about the meaning of fiction. He may or may not approve of the critical method I have developed or agree with the conclusions I have come to about Henry James, but he is nevertheless responsible for having originally set my mind in motion and given it the impetus to undertake and complete my exegesis of James's fiction.

Acknowledgment is also due to the firms of CHARLES SCRIBNER'S SONS, HARPER AND BROTHERS, and MACMILLAN AND COMPANY of New York and London, respectively, for permission to use the sentences quoted from Henry James's *Notes on Novelists*, *Essays in London and Elsewhere*, and *French Poets and Novelists*.

OSBORN ANDREAS

Cobden, Illinois
March, 1948

CONTENTS

———

The great question as to a poet or a novelist is, How does he feel about life? What, in the last analysis, is his philosophy? When vigorous writers have reached maturity we are at liberty to look in their works for some expression of a total view of the world that they have been so actively observing. This is the most interesting thing their works offer us. Details are interesting in proportion as they contribute to make it clear.—Henry James, *French Poets And Novelists*.

. . . indeed, it may be said that the study of connections is the recognized function of intelligent criticism . . . they become still more interesting as we note their coincidences and relations with other works . . . the plot thickens, the whole spectacle expands.—Henry James, *Essays In London And Elsewhere*.

His subject is always, like the subjects of all first-rate men, primarily an idea. . . .—*Op. cit.*

. . . for is it not the very function of criticism and the sign of its intelligence to acquit itself honorably in embarrassing conditions and track the idea with patience just in proportion as it is elusive?—*Op. cit.*

. . . if it is interesting to be puzzled to a certain extent by what an action, placed before us, is designed to show or to signify, so we require for this refined amusement at least the sense that some general idea is represented. We must feel it present.—Henry James, *Notes On Novelists*.

Highly attaching as indeed the game might be, of inquiring as to the centre of interest or the sense of the whole in. . . .—*Op. cit.*

. . . though certain betrayals of a controlling idea and a pointed intention do comparatively gleam out of the last two fictions named.—*Op. cit.*

We surely wonder more what it may all propose to mean. . . .—*Op. cit.* We ask ourselves what *Sinister Street* may mean as a whole in spite of our sense of being brushed from the first by a hundred subordinate purposes, the succession and alternation of which seem to make after a fashion a plan, and which, though full of occasional design, yet fail to gather themselves for application or to converge to an idea.—*Op. cit.*

INTRODUCTION

HENRY JAMES was the novelist of consciousness, not the historian of consciences. Levels of awareness and qualities of consciousness were his subject; good and evil entered his theme only as they contributed to a clearing or a clouding, to a dulling or a sharpening, of the consciousness and the sensibilities. He once (in the paper entitled, "Is There A Life After Death?" *In After Days*, Harper Bros., 1910) stated that consciousness, the creative awareness of things, was the highest good he could conceive of, and that it was the business of the artist to carry the field of consciousness further and further, in fact, to promote the accumulation of the very treasure itself of consciousness.

It is this interest of James in the experience of consciousness itself that entitles us to define James as a great humanist, that exonerates him from the charge of pure and unprincipled aestheticism, and that furnishes the clue for his manner of deep and passionate participation in life. James was no cold, unmoved and dispassionate spectator of the human world. There were certain things in human nature that he cared for, deeply and fiercely, and certain things that he hated; his art was consecrated to humanistic ends and consequently is charged with humanistic meanings and implications.

He deplored certain styles of human behavior because they deadened the sensibilities of both the actor and him acted upon, and he esteemed others because they enhanced the

1

power of the individual to rise to greater heights of awareness. He considered the cultivation of consciousness to be the most rewarding activity of man, the greatest privilege of life, and the supreme affirmation of man's essential nature.

The fiction of Henry James is an attempt to define the most conscious man. James believed that, since the contents of consciousness are the behavior of man, certain kinds of behavior enhance the vividness of consciousness and the richness of life while others depress the action and impair the limpidity of mind. His novels and stories are a search for and an exposure of the kind of behavior which muddies that limpidity and an analytic but embodied presentation of the kind of behavior that promotes it.

James's primary interest was the experience of being alive. He was interested in ethics, in ideas, in science, in economics, in politics, in civilization, in history, in love, only insofar as these were factors affecting the one great value: intensity of consciousness. The one most universal thing common to all human beings, past, present and future, is the sense of being alive—and this, in a word, is James's theme, the central subject of all his fiction. Some people are more alive than others, and it is in the power of human beings to stimulate or to benumb not only other people's sense of life but also their own. James's fiction holds up to our view persons in the act of achieving more sense of life, persons murdering it in themselves and others, and persons nourishing the sentient principle in the people about them.

The drama of the struggle of consciousness for complete awareness is peopled in James's fiction with men and women whose contending styles of behavior recur wherever human beings, whatever their historical era or their race or their level in the economic or social strata of their time, establish interacting social relationships. A James novel does not deal with a problem of a specific historical time or of a specific social class or even of a specific civilized area of the earth's populated surface; it deals with interacting character-qualities as ancient as Neanderthal man and as contemporary as this morning's breakfast. These qualities necessarily wear the garment of the time and place in which James lived—but in themselves they are ageless and classless.

I

James saw what is in human beings that smothers their minds and reduces their clarity of vision; he saw too what is required of him who would be mentally awake, commanding the power and exercising the gift of consciousness. James was the implacable analyst who pursued into its myriads of incarnations, exposing the oneness of identity under its many guises, that propensity in human beings to which he attributed all blunting of sensibility: the propensity to acts of intervention in the lives of other people. It was for the destruction of this propensity—and for the augmenting of its opposite: the impulse to tender and sympathetic carefulness with the expansive potentialities of other people—that James strove, creating a body of fiction as diligently wrought as Flaubert's and as large in quantity as Balzac's.

What James principally saw in life was the harm which people inflict—not only on others but on themselves—by deeds of emotional cannibalism. The almost ubiquitous, vicious and deep-rooted illusion that one's own life can get sustenance from an emotional feeding on the lives of others was the object of his lifelong attack. Not only does intervention in the lives of others fail to allay the appetite of the intervener, it also—and this is its chief deadliness—poisons the sources of feeling. It deprives the assaulter of sensitive power and it paralyzes the sensory activity of the assaulted. Intervention was, in James's conception, a means to an unworthy end which reacts to the damage of its user.

James isolated several different modes of intervention which are identical in essence and variant only in degree. They possess in common a violence directed against the autonomy of the individual, an intent to manipulate the lives of others and a purposive interference with their behavior.

The mildest-seeming and yet one of the most vicious of these modes of intervention is opinion, opinion itself, about the private lives of other people. James felt that not only opinion publicly expressed but also opinion privately held about the conduct, particularly the moral conduct, of others is an affront to the right of every individual to base his conduct on the needs of his nature. Opinion about the private conduct of other people is by its very nature based on evidence insufficient to any definitive conclusion and is therefore invariably epistemologically unsound; undermining the sense of truth by violating the grounds of knowledge. That person, therefore, who consents to the lodgment in his mind of an opinion about the private conduct of his neighbor is more damaged by that consent than is the person about whom the opinion is held. This penumbra knowledge to which people give credence, sometimes in the form of mob opinion and sometimes in the form of secret moral snobbery, is in James's view an intolerable indignity and one to be mercilessly expunged from the face of the earth.

Another and more overt mode of intervention that James identified and scorned is that of outright meddling in others' lives. This kind of interference is sometimes well-intentioned, sometimes merely heedless, but more often maliciously and acquisitively officious. In James's stories meddlers range from the nuisance category through the pest type to that of the predacious well-wisher. They possess in common the offensive trait of assuming that they know better than their victims what kind of life the latter should lead. The error of the busybody is germane to that of the disciplinarian: blindness to the fact that people are like plants that can only be watered, not touched.

Another form of aggression a shade more severe than meddling is parasitism. James conceived of parasitism, whether it be financial or emotional, as a total loss for the human parasite, since his resort to this means of escape from his natural destiny cheats him of the fruits of self-expansion in the terms of his internal nature, and as a mitigated loss for the host, since his consent to the presence of the parasite derives from a considerateness worthy in itself but unfortunate in its object. The helplessness of the host, his paralysis before the aggressive parasite, baffled and annoyed James because the power to support the parasite indicated the presence of reserves of sensibility, immobilized and made sterile, the creative exercise of which would have so enlarged the consciousness of its possessor. Pathos, however, rather than tragedy, is the dominant note of James's stories of parasitism.

The next more violent form of intervention is coercion. James's feeling of revulsion for any coercive act is almost mystical. He often traces a chain of tragic events back to one original act of coercion, a fateful deed as immutably tragic in its remotest consequences as a Greek sin. James always permits the blight to fall on so many additional and innocent people as well as on the person coerced, and he does not spare us one turn in tracing the path of the evil deed. He accents the intrinsic evilness of coercion by usually giving the coercer himself a creditable motive, thereby lifting the narrative from the villain-victim category to the true tragic level. James brooked no compromise on this issue: coercion was to him always and forever and in whatever guise an unmitigated bitterness.

The final and purest form of emotional cannibalism is exploitation. The disrespect for human individuality, even his own, in that person who makes a base and illegitimate use of other people for his own advantage and profit was, in James's scheme of values, the supreme source of evil. The evil itself was loss of consciousness, and since consciousness was the fruit of free development in the line of one's own idiosyncrasy, interference in that free development to such a degree as to amount to exploitation was the seed of evil. Indulgence in looting, James insisted, was not confined to the savage tribes who waged aggressive war; it is extensively practiced today in personal and emotional relationships between presumably civilized human beings, and it is the cardinal sin which people commit against one another.

A variant of the exploitation theme in James's fiction is that of revenge. Revenge is that form of exploitation which fancies that retaliation serves the cause of justice, whereas, in fact, it merely serves the cause of self-aggrandizement at the expense of someone who deserves to pay. Revenge and exploitation are essentially identical in that each seeks emotional satisfaction in the bending of another being to one's own purposes. The false assumption at the heart of these two forms of behavior, as well as of all other variants of emotional cannibalism, is that there is profit of any kind to be derived from intervention in the lives of other people.

II

The obverse of this theme, the positive statement of which emotional cannibalism is the negative counterpart, asserts the supreme value for consciousness of a constant, unremitting, and sympathetic consideration of the feelings of others. One's own capacity for awareness, one's own sensibility, is increased by a study of, a respect for, and a nurturing of the sensibilities and awarenesses of other people. We grow, not by tearing other people down, but by building them up.

One of the approaches to acquaintance with this law of conduct is encountered by people who suddenly see that the revenge which they are about to accomplish will really avail them nothing. Revenge forsworn appears in James's fiction as a phenomenon of enlightenment, forbearance unexpectedly

7

presenting itself to the vengeance seeker as more desirable than the sight of the opponent's humiliation. The suddenness of the revelation gives it a mystical character, but James always bases it on experience: long-plotted revenge, upon reaching the threshold of its goal, stays its hand. The longed-for and long striven-for act inexplicably loses its anticipated savor. This event is a first intimation of a truth deeply bedded in the logic of behavior.

Another approach to this principle of conduct which James uses in his fiction is that of regret and repentance for an act of intervention in the life of another, after longer life and reflection have yielded understanding. People severely schooled by the consequences of their actions sometimes do learn, James contends, the true nature of the damage they have inflicted on themselves. James shows these people achieving awareness, but at a costly rate—often too costly for survival.

The truly superior persons, however, according to James's test for quality, are those whose native disposition impels them to maintain a scrupulous respect for the personal rights and sensibilities of all people, even those foreign in kind. People whose sensibilities we do not share, people who have predilections for strange classes or levels of phenomena and who may or may not respond to the values we ourselves cherish, are as entitled to our careful regard as are people of our own kind. Their humanity—not their class or race or even their personal quality—is what we are beholden to. Kindness to and noninterference with others is a principle of behavior which applies to all individuals, not just to some kindred spirits, and violation of the principle, even with reference to persons we do not understand or like, will make callous the soul and harden the sensibility.

In fact, the ideal person, in James's scheme of human values, is the one who knows—and acts in accordance with his knowledge—that compassion is the clue to conduct. It is to this theme that he devoted his greatest novel. The way of life which will enrich the consciousness, swiftly make one aware of and vibrant to more and more facets of the experience of living, is the one which subordinates all other emotions and desires and purposes to the emotion of compassion. Tenderness towards other people is the true grace, and its greatest fruit is the power to fathom, with pellucid clarity of mind, the world we live in.

This is not to be confused with humanitarianism. James was certainly no humanitarian. James was looking for a way of behavior which would enable him, or anyone, to see and understand the world the way it really is. His basic search was for truth, and the reason he wanted truth was that it, and it only, fills the mind. Error shrinks the mind, while truth enlarges it. Compassion was the device, the methodology, by means of which one purified one's sensibility and perfected it as one's instrument of perception.

III

Skepticism as to the value of personal love, romantic and sexual, in galvanizing the consciousness was, however, a characteristic Jamesian theme, and one which undoubtedly accounts for the cool reception bestowed on many of his novels by the general public. In his earliest stories, as well as in his very latest, love is presented as a mysterious malady, as a rival to the self-discipline required for the achievement of a career, and as a stimulus to the acquisitive rather than to the generous impulses in men and women. Furthermore, love miscarried is deadly; the risks of and the penalties for defeat are so great and the benefits of success so doubtful that the emotion is too dangerous to merit a commitment that is not wrenched from one. And the difficulty of disentangling the economic aspect of marriage from the emotional aggravated James's distrust.

James's principal objection, however, to the emotion of personal love was that it dulled the sense of truth. A man in love is not a completely self-reliant person, looking at the world through his own eyes: he is necessarily conditioned by the hostage which he has given to happiness. In a manner of speaking, every lover is a liar, simply because his every thought and emotion is oriented with reference, not primarily to accurate and just appraisal of the external world, but to the safety and exaltation of the loved object. James did not minimize the power of love and he did not deny that it filled the consciousness. His complaint was rather that it transfixed the attention of its victim, circumscribed and restricted his field of observation, and rendered his testimony invalid on any subject but that of his own feelings and those of his loved object. And even on these two subjects his testimony is untrustworthy because his allegiance goes primarily, not to objective truth, but to the state of his relation at the moment to the loved one. The solipsism, the anti-social character of love offended James because it removed each pair of lovers into a charmed circle wherein all activity other than preoccupation with themselves was arrested and immobilized.

James's final comment on love was that it usually turns into some form of emotional cannibalism, vicious in its rapacity and possessiveness. Both the lover and the beloved prey on each other's emotions—and to what end? Everything stands still while the lovers fight it out, and exhaustion and depletion are the only outcome. The lovers may think that they have lived—but James does not (or does any other observer?) think so. James conceives of living as an accumulation of consciousness and as a continually accelerating power to use one's consciousness; since personal love, romantic and sexual, does not further this process, James regards it as more of a deterrent than a help to the full life.

IV

One of the positive helps to a quickened consciousness is a sense of the past, and of this enduring agency of enlightenment James was very fond. An intensified awareness of the present moment can be gained, he often demonstrates, by attempting to reach back imaginatively and relive past time. Substance is added to the present by awareness of the past, one's personal past as well as that of one's generation and its progenitors. It is not the historians' past, the past of recorded history, of which James was enamoured; it is the past yet tangibly present here in our midst in the form of architecture and furnishings of domestic use and traditional ways of living. The continuity of the present with the past, the perspective interrelation between the present and the immediate and the remoter past, observable to the senses, is a resource ready for the uses of an expanding capacity for life. The extension of consciousness to include what we are apt to think of as dead and gone, instead of diverting attention from today's real world, fertilizes the current day by, paradoxically, emphasizing its durability in time.

James was acutely aware, however, of the danger of romanticizing the past. The past was for one's present use, but it was not to be employed as a substitute for present living. His ideal—complete consciousness—was of course, necessarily, a matter of the immediate present, the current instant in time; the presence of the past, to enrich the present moment, was what he wanted: not a translation into the past, to evade the present. Many of his stories were written to expose the misuse of the past, to show that the past must be exorcized before it can be effectively put to present uses. To place oneself in relation to as large a segment of time as possible was not, for James, a looking backward to or a nostalgia for the past; it was one of the ways by means of which one enhanced the intensity of, and gained a more complete perception of, the present.

V

Another Jamesian theme, subordinate but integral to his central subject, has to do with the conflict between two standards of value, the one implicit in the artistic homage and endeavor, the other in the lure of power and position.

People who are activated by the former standard reserve their deepest respect for the truth and beauty of the aesthetic consciousness, while the latter deem the greatest rewards in life to be those connected with eminence of worldly station. This basic conflict pervades every human activity. It marks the line of deepest cleavage between people and even between the two principal segments within a single personality. The instinct of workmanship versus mass production. The heretic suffering torture and death in loyalty to an idea versus the orthodox cardinal secure in his sinecure. The satisfaction of a disinterested curiosity of the mind versus the timeserver suborned by fleshpots. The concept of the great lady versus the woman of wealth. The just man versus the rich man. The creative imagination versus the acquisitive instinct. The considerate person versus the busybody. The laissez faire versus the parasitic and the predatory principle in human relations. Sympathy and understanding versus the impulse to conquer. The desire to see versus the desire to shine. The impulse to do the difficult and unremunerative but internally satisfying thing in line with one's idiosyncrasy versus the urge to do the easy and cheap for its great material reward. Freedom for the mind versus security for the body.

The individual formations of this conflict are infinite in number, and the second term of the above sample oppositions represents, of course, the official dominant philosophy regnant in every age and society. In assailing it, James isolated for attack the very inner citadel of special privilege: that desire in the heart of man to domineer in some degree over his fellow man, the belief that self-fulfillment can be found in the exercise of dominion over others. James holds, on the other hand, that the essential nature of the kind of activity in which the artist is engaged implies the existence of values contradictory to the official ones and, furthermore, capable of general application and use.

VI

Another object of attack on James's part was the sheltered life. The notion that there is something harmful in experience, that too much experience coarsens the sensibilities or tarnishes the mind, is one that James resolutely combatted. He attacked restrictions on experience, and he condemned the fear of exposure to too great a quantity of experience.

In the interest of enhanced awareness he advocated, on the other hand, an acceptance of all experiences within one's reach. Every possible variety of experience is, in James's view, grist for the mill of the most conscious man. The experience of living is the material upon which the consciousness works in its self-refining and self-tempering exertions, and therefore the exclusion of any aspect or kind of experience can only result in a less finely tempered consciousness. To refuse experience is to refuse life itself: to this antithesis of the ivory tower James gave support by making it the theme of several novels and stories.

It was the development of this facet of James's outlook that led him into conflict with the moral conventions, social taboos, and class barriers of his time. His fiction consistently manifests sympathy for the Rousseauistic and romantic belief in the essentially good strength of human nature, because he always represents as desirable the success of an expanding personality in its attempts to break through barriers which have been set up to protect it from what has been considered to be evil. These barriers may have been established by parents or guardians or by society, or they may have been erected by the personality within itself, through fear, to protect it against evils which may be either fancied or real. But James always wants the evil to be grappled with, even when the encounter may have a doubtful outcome.

This sympathy with the expanding personality possesses a long history. It began with Rousseau, became the central tenet of the Romantic movement in nineteenth-century culture, and reached its completest expression in our American social order. We in America, for instance, believe that the public school, where no protective barrier exists between bad and good children, is preferable to the private school, to which children from "good" families only are admitted. James concurs in this American predilection for the sweeping away of all protective barriers. In fact, he emphasizes multiplicity of relations as a principal characteristic of the kind of living which produces the complete person.

James attacked, in this truly American and Romantic tradition, that convention of thought which assumes that the desirable person is the one into whose life has entered only selected experiences, discriminated contacts, sheltered relations. James fought against censorship of every kind: of publishers against literature, of the old against the young, of class against class, of restrictive moral convention against free-ranging experimental living. The American temper in James, reacting to contact with the aristocratic ordering of life in Europe and England (and its pale afterlife in New England), made his gorge rise at the spectacle of maze and network devised to corral the behavior of man.

VII

The removal of fences from the enclosures in which people lived gave rise, however, to another problem: the mystery of personal identity. The convenience of a fenced-off area was that it enabled one to identify the people who lived there. James's advocacy of multiplicity of relations to life obliterated the easy categories by means of which people are customarily defined, and he found himself then facing the problem of what in themselves people really are. It became necessary for him to find some deeper principle of definition.

In search of this principle he reconsidered his concept of the most conscious man, and in a corollary of that concept he found the answer to his problem. If the complete man is the most conscious one, and if increase of consciousness is brought about by study of the sensibilities of other people, then the contents of consciousness are the behavior of man— and here we have our principle of definition. People are what they do: not what they do for a living but what they do in the sensibilities of people who observe them.

The peculiar virtue of this emphasis which James gives to the interdependance, for very existence, of all conscious entities is that it makes this a social world; it eats the heart out of the solipsistic egoist who lightly thinks, as he elbows his way through life, that other people are not important to him. The sensibilities of other people are the food by which we live: if we injure them, we rot the food we live by; if we let them be what they are, they will grow like manna for our use. James's solution to the mystery of personal identity is, therefore, a part of the pattern itself of his central theme, although the posing of the question was a consequence of his romantic attack on the sequestration of experience.

VIII

Some of James's short stories are like pools quarried near the banks of the channel he dredged to carry the main stream of his themes. They are thoughts allied to, and consistent with, his principal thought, but they are not an integral part of his structure of meaning. These stories examine false values and endeavor to destroy them. If the development of one's consciousness is the supreme value, then other values which men have made supreme in their lives must be shown to be inferior or false.

Fame, social position, cosmopolitanism, moral appearances, nationalistic patriotism, the preservation of personal beauty, and pretense to talent: these are the false values he examines. All of them possess a characteristic in common: they have to do with an exaltation of the self in the eyes of other people. In this they radically differ from James's supreme value. The more conscious person necessarily welcomes accession of consciousness in less conscious people, because that in turn enhances his own. But fame is jealous of rivals; social position depends on exclusion of others;

cosmopolitanism loses its glamour if everybody travels; moral appearances are made to seem more righteous by the exposure of others' sins; nationalistic patriotism battens on the mal-practices of hostile nations; the preservation of personal beauty is made more remarkable by the rapidity with which the comeliness of others declines; and pretenders to talent are exposed to shame by the emergence of real talent.

All of the false values depend in some degree on the re-pression of other people; therefore, like the forms of emo-tional cannibalism, they are potent and hostile forces counter-posed to those which nourish man's capacity for greater awareness.

IX

In three of James's stories—very short ones—the inter-national theme provides the subject. The source of dramatic tension in this small group of stories lies in characteristic differences between national schools of opinion, notions common to a nation regarding the proper relation between society and the individual. Clashes between individuals traceable to differences in national character are, of course, necessarily shallower and less lasting in time than clashes due to differences in human character, since the qualities that pertain to a human being cover a far wider range than those which pertain to an American or an Englishman; therefore they are given but scant direct treatment in the body of James's fiction.

These three stories possess in common an emphasis upon the beneficial effect observably attributable to the loosening,

in America, of the bonds which, in Europe, society fastens
upon the individual. James approvingly notes that in America the marrying couple, rather than the husband's family
clan, as in Europe, is the social unit; that class distinctions
in America are more horizontal and in Europe more vertical;
and that the type-American does not require in his pleasures
that quality of exclusiveness which to the type-European is
any pleasure's chief fillip. A freer flowering of the individual,
James's desideratum, is the natural consequence of these
American improvements upon the European concept of
society's hegemony over the persons that compose it.

X

One considerable group of James's stories has no tributary
connection whatever with either his main or his supplemen-
tary themes. Apart from this group, and from the small group
dealing with international contrasts, all of James's stories
and novels have some bearing on, and exist in some relation
to, the central subject of his work: accession or depletion of
consciousness.

The principal characters in these residual stories, which
are so separate in kind from the bulk of his writing, are
creative artists. These are the people, in James's view, who
have solved the problem of consciousness. It is the very
nature of their characteristic activity to carry on a continual
exploration of consciousness, and therefore there is no need
to teach them that more and more consciousness is the aim
of existence, that the sympathetic study of others' consciousness will enhance their own, or that behavior has its adverse

and its favorable bearings on consciousness. On the other hand, to have used the artist as a fictional character to illustrate his central theme would have lessened the force of that theme's impact on the nonartist public, as does any definition of the simpler in terms of the more complex.

James's stories of creative artists are, then, keyed in a much lower tone and possess a much slighter structure of meaning than that greater group of stories which carry his deepest thought. What these stories say is merely that it is the responsibility of the reading public to give the artist the attention he needs, that it is the responsibility of the literary critic to give the artist a thoughtful rather than a cursory perusal, that the created work instead of the artist's private life is the deserving object of attention, that the critic's business is to examine what the creative artist has done rather than to speculate on what he might have done had he been a different sort of man. These stories are in essence admonitory epistles addressed by a practicing creative artist to the critical reading public, and as such they are of the nature of prologues to his important work.

CONCLUSION

This completes the preliminary survey and statement of the themes to be found in James's fiction. That these are the meanings which James placed in his stories will be substantiated in the following chapters of this book by means of concise interpretive summaries (not synopses) of all his stories and novels except those which appeared only in magazines. In an attempt to find out as fully and precisely as possible what the stories say, I have condensed each one into a précis-like vignette, from a perspective in which only the most outstanding lineaments appear, so that the essential meaning, undistracted by minor plot elements, may be thrust out into high relief. My intention has been to strip from the plots everything but the basic timbers and rafters of the story structure so that the silhouette in profile will bring into view the contour, direction, and significant shape of the story's sense.

The order in which the stories are considered is not chronological but thematic, since the meaning of one James story usually becomes clear only by the light which is cast on it by another or by a group of others. James's stories and novels, thematically inspected, naturally fall into ten major groups, corresponding to the ten chapters of this book; and each story in a group casts one ray of illumination on that facet of James's theme to which the group is devoted. To make the full circuit of all the facets is to become intimately acquainted with one of the minds, most remarkable for power and grace, which has—unobtrusively but ineffaceably, through its influence on other artists—effected a deep change in the intellectual and artistic chemistry of all men since his time.

Chapter One

EMOTIONAL CANNIBALISM

HENRY JAMES published in book form one hundred and twenty-five separate works of fiction. The largest single group of these studies in human behavior is composed of those which develop the numerous aspects of his theme of emotional cannibalism. This term signifies that tendency in human nature to obtain emotional nourishment from indulgence in acts of aggression on other human beings. James's observation of human behavior yielded a diagnosis at once original and creative: that an intimate though subterranean link subsists between an individual's choice of emotional nourishment and his clarity of mind, that the former conditions the latter rather than the reverse, and that therefore it is within our own power to gain or destroy acuteness of sensibility in ourselves and in others.

Consciousness is dimmed and sensibility is anesthetized in the aggressor and in his victim, by any act of interference with others which is motivated by an egoistic desire for emotional gratification. James, of course, did not start out as a young writer with this thought full-blown; on the contrary, he had to feel his way towards it as he wrote story after story of intervention. One can see it gradually taking shape in James's mind as one reads through the earlier stories and those of his middle years to the later productions of the mature artist. The idea is implicit in embryo, however, in his very earliest work.

I

We will consider first that group of James's stories which treats of the mildest-seeming kind of intervention: the indulgence in opinion about the private lives of other people. On this subject James wrote nine stories, the first one in 1869 and the last in 1900.

The Baron de Bergerac, in *Gabrielle De Bergerac* (1869), guardian of his sister Gabrielle, permits himself to be misled by appearances into forming an opinion as to his sister's relations with her tutor, Pierre Coquelin. It is true that Gabrielle and Pierre were in love with each other, but Gabrielle, out of respect for her brother's wishes, had resolved to dismiss Pierre. The Baron, however, takes the unwarranted step of cruelly, unjustly, and publicly accusing Gabrielle of having become Pierre's clandestine mistress. This act of interference so violates Gabrielle's sense of private dignity that it incites her to reverse her previous decision. The liberty which her brother had taken with her moral autonomy as a human being destroys her allegiance to him as the head of her family. Freed from her guardian by his opinionated assault on her integrity, she feels justified in eloping with Pierre, whom she marries.

In the following year (1870) James wrote the story named *Travelling Companions*, in which public opinion plays a somewhat different role. The unspoken but nevertheless conscious desire of two lovers for matrimony is nearly thwarted by the misunderstanding which a snickering public opinion precipitates between them. The mischance of missing the last train home from a nearby town, to which they had paid an afternoon sight-seeing visit, compels them to remain overnight in the strange town together. Upon their return the following day, they notice that the general public in their own town had remarked the incident, drawing the usual invidious conclusions. When, soon thereafter, the young man asks the girl to marry him, she gives him a negative answer, fearing that his proposal was prompted mainly by his belief that she felt herself to have been compromised by him in the eyes of the public. Their union in marriage is delayed a year by public notice having been taken of their private actions.

In *Madame De Mauves* (1875) James again emphasizes the essential immorality of any attempt to order other people's lives for them. Euphemia Cleve, after she had suffered for four or five years from her husband's neglect and infidelities, falls in love with Longmore and he with her. The affair is progressing nicely and the two would have become lovers had not Euphemia's husband, Richard de Mauves, and his sister, Marie, losing patience at the slowness with which the situation was developing, fatally taken it upon themselves to explicitly urge the enamoured pair to go ahead and have an affair. This violation of her personal and private independence of decision, this public notice taken of a personal matter so offends Euphemia that she dismisses Longmore, the one man who could have made her happy. The source of this tragedy was Richard's and Marie's lack of delicacy, their want of genuine regard for Euphemia's and Longmore's feelings.

Daisy Miller, in the story of that name (1878), dies from the effects of indiscretions she is impelled to commit out of exasperation at the penalties exacted of her by people who express too openly their disapproval of her minor and innocent infractions of the social code. Public opinion had unjustly accused her of being too intimate with Giovanelli, and when Frederick Winterbourne, the man she loved, instead of defending her or at least merely laughing with her at public opinion for its gullibility, scolded her for not being more careful of appearances, Daisy recklessly spent an hour in the miasmal Coliseum moonlight with Giovanelli. There she caught a fever of which she died, apparently a victim of her own impetuous and shallow rashness, but more truly a victim of the cowardly and petty inconsiderateness of public opinion. Daisy typifies those hasty and choleric but generous and good people whose first impulse, in quick reply to the sting and bruise of a cynical public's false accusation, is to continue, in a flagrantly exaggerated form, the conduct for which they have been criticized. The folly of this type-response to public censure is less blameworthy, in James's view, than a public expression of opinion on private conduct.

In *An International Episode* (1878), the relation between Bessie Alden and Lord Lambeth, which might well have developed into a warm and deep friendship if not into marriage, was ruined by friends and relatives who did not possess sufficient restraint and considerate feeling to refrain from forming and betraying opinions about the relation. Public opinion, exercising itself in its too usual role of speculator on matters which are none of its business, is the villain of this narrative; and it is embodied here in Bessie's sister, Mrs. Westgate, and in Lord Lambeth's best friend, Percy Beaumont.

Count Otto Vogelstein, in *Pandora* (1885), lost the girl he loved because of his exaggerated deference to public opinion. Pandora Day excited him the very first day he saw her and his shipboard acquaintance with her developed into love almost instantaneously. He let the relation drop, however, when he was informed by Mrs. Dangerfield that the Day family was not regarded as socially possible by the discriminating. Two years later, when he sees her again and realizes that he has been in love with her all that time, she appears as the friend of Mrs. Steuben, whose social position is irreproachable. Pandora, however, is now engaged to marry a D. F. Bellamy, whose appointment as minister to Holland has just been announced. Otto realizes too late that he might have won her for himself had he not been so craven as to permit public opinion to deflect him.

Laura Wing, in *A London Life* (1888), struggles with all her fierce, little, intolerant, virginal, eighteen-year-old might to keep the elements of her environment from shifting about and casting her adrift. And in doing so she expresses all the conservatism of youth, the resentful bewilderment with which youth, unacquainted with the passions of maturity, sees its elders play fast and loose with the *status quo*. Laura lives with her sister and brother-in-law, Selina and Lionel Berrington, whose marriage is disintegrating. The prospect of a scandal and divorce terrifies Laura, because she fears that Mr. Wendover, her suitor, will not propose marriage if Selina stains the family name in a divorce court. She cannot understand why Selina finds her lover more necessary to her than her husband, her two little children, and her place in society, nor why Lionel can't let other women alone. She pleads with each of them, separately, embarrassing them with her passionate innocence, and winning for her pains little more than a baffled feeling that they think her a prig.

On the night that Selina bolts with her lover, Laura is impelled, in desperation, to make certain advances to Wendover in the hope that he will be stimulated to offer an immediate proposal of marriage. But he does not catch the point quickly enough, and Laura, in rage and shame and self-disgust, runs away from him. For the want of a faculty of sympathetic imagination concerning the personal situations of specific individuals known to her, and especially for the want of courage to brave an adverse public opinion, Laura will require an inordinate amount of hard experience, if the maturing process is ever to have its way with her.

Grace Mavis, in *The Patagonia* (1888), is driven to suicide by the addition to her other hardly bearable troubles of the unfeeling Grundyism, the impertinently censorious and publicly expressed opinions of her neighbors concerning her moral conduct. Urged on by the insistence of her family to accept the invitation of her fiancé of several year's standing to join him in Europe now that he can afford to marry her, she sails on the Patagonia, reluctant though she is to marry a man whom she can scarcely remember. On shipboard she meets Jasper Nettlepoint, a wealthy and worldly young man who had been in her girlhood a romantic object to her, idolized from afar. He amuses himself in her company, spending almost his entire time with her. Grace falls in love with him, while knowing that he would not marry her and knowing too that she must marry her fiancé when she lands in Europe. This she would probably have been able to go through with, if she had been permitted to have her little romance with Jasper unnoticed. The other travelers on the ship, however, spread scandal and gossip, and Grace is finally cold-shouldered into hopelessness. She disappears overboard during the night, a victim of the conspicuously unsympathetic treatment of the Mrs. Grundys of this world.

Bertram Braddle, in *The Great Condition* (1899), finds himself unable to face a possibly disparaging and derisive public opinion regarding Mrs. Damerel, the woman he loves and wants to marry. Worried because she has lived her entire life, previous to his meeting her, in a far country, where her husband and child had died, he makes the mistake of asking her point-blank whether there has ever been anything discreditable in her life. To this she gives the only answer open to a self-respecting woman: that she will tell him six months after their marriage. This is "the great condition" which he cannot accept. He goes to the far country to investigate her past, whereupon Mrs. Damerel cancels her engagement to marry him. She marries Henry Chilver who, says Mrs. Damerel, "thinks me what he finds me."

The unwarranted impingement of public opinion on private conduct is the thematic element common to these nine stories. In every case, damage or disaster comes to innocent people by the agency of wanton and gratuitous opinion on the part of people who need not have busied themselves about the matter at all. Interference by opinion is therein shown to be one of the vicious forms of emotional cannibalism.

II

Intervention takes the form of outright meddling in another group of stories, six in number. The meddler makes it his business to interfere by an overt deed in matters which are none of his concern. Opinion has eventuated in action. In these stories, the aggressor is usually someone who enjoys a much closer personal relation to his victim than does his counterpart in the stories of opinion. It is this personal relation which furnishes him the grounds of his presumption and which affords him the advantage which he presses. Defense against this type of aggression is of course exceedingly difficult to contrive, since the personal tie exacts of the victim an abundant and enduring tolerance for his antagonist.

In James's earliest story on this theme, *The Romance Of Certain Old Clothes* (1868), the transgressor is a wife who harries her husband into violating a promise that he had given his first wife on her deathbed. Rosalind's punishment for this forward and envious act of interference in her husband's obligations was death—at the hands of the first wife's ghost.

Bernard Longueville, in *Confidence* (1879), makes the apparently innocent and generous mistake of accepting the invitation of his friend, Gordon Wright, to meddle in his (Gordon Wright's) life by advising him whether or not to marry Angela Vivian. Bernard's punishment for this indiscretion is that he comes very near losing the girl he finally marries and also the friendship of Gordon, his closest lifelong intimate. If Bernard had refrained from any attempt at the slightest interference in the relation between Angela and

Gordon, he would have saved all three of them from a great many heartaches.

Morris Townsend, in *Washington Square* (1880), cheats his fiancée, Catherine Sloper, of her birthright of natural development into a normal wife—her innate destiny—and in so doing he becomes an incarnation of what to James is supremely evil. Morris jilted Catherine when he discovered that her father, Austin Sloper, who had rightly judged him to be a fortune hunter, would disinherit her should she marry him. Her subsequent refusal to marry anyone else, together with the knowledge that her father had been in the right and she in the wrong, worked like a blight eating into the remainder of her life. She had voluntarily given up her father and his fortune in order to marry Morris, and then Morris had reneged. Her father, on his deathbed, disinherited her anyway, when she refused to promise never to marry Morris at any future time. Morris did come back after Austin's death, but Catherine would have nothing to do with him. She therefore lost not only Morris but also her father and her patrimony as well as her desire to be a wedded wife. The end result of accepting her state was that she remained a jilted woman all her life, an example of the crippling effect unscrupulous meddlers can exercise on the lives of innocent people.

Kate Julian, in *Owen Wingrave* (1893), through her failure to attempt a sympathetic understanding of her lover's point of view in his quarrel with his family on the issue of whether he should chuck or continue a military career, makes the mistake of meddling in the quarrel, and thereby unwittingly becomes an agent of death to the man she is engaged to marry. Pressure by the family on a son to engage in a career not to his liking, interference on the part of the family in the son's choice of occupation, brings tragic death to Owen Wingrave.

In *The Death Of The Lion* (1894), Neil Paraday, a quiet and retiring novelist who had, to his bewilderment, suddenly become famous in his late middle age, is exploited by Mrs. Wimbush, a social impresario who uses him to add lustre and reputation to her drawing room. The managing Mrs. Wimbush browbeats the timid Paraday, whose quiet bachelor life as a novelist has not taught him how to cope with high-handed society women, into staying indefinitely at her country house to be the principal ornament to attract other guests. He is made very unhappy by the situation, as he wants to exercise his genius, instead of wasting his time in small talk. Mrs. Wimbush does not understand or care about his writing; she cares only for his publicity value. At a final week-end houseparty, Paraday's strength gives out: he catches pneumonia and dies. In the subsequent confusion the manuscript of his last great novel is irretrievably lost. What the world can ill afford to lose is to Mrs. Wimbush, ironically, no great loss, but merely the death of another social lion.

Mora Montravers, in the story of that name (1909), punishes her aunt and foster mother, Jane Traffle, for her conceited, insulting, and crude intervention in Mora's private life. Upon reaching the age of twenty-one, Mora moves out of her foster parents' house and takes temporary lodging in a screened-off corner of Walter Puddick's studio located in the Greenwich Village of London. Mora had disliked her aunt's house because it contained no evidences of any artistic or intellectual interest, its prevailing tone being, on the other hand, stuffy, bourgeois, middle-class and suburban. Since her own interests are, like those of her friends, artistic and literary, Mora had decided that she should live in the vicinity of people more like herself.

Her Aunt Jane is of course scandalized and convinced that Mora is simply Walter Puddick's mistress. Upon meeting Walter and finding that he is a presentable young man, Jane decides that a marriage of the guilty pair would retrieve the situation and offers to settle a life income of four hundred and fifty pounds per year on Walter if he marries Mora. Mora has had no intention of marrying Walter, but she is so incensed at her aunt for her effrontery in acting upon the assumption that she is Walter's mistress that she promptly marries Walter, gets the money from her aunt, and then— never having lived with him as his wife—signs the entire income over to Walter and divorces him.

In each one of these stories, an acquaintance or friend or relative oversteps the bounds of that jurisdiction to which he is entitled by his personal relation to an individual. Rosalind, Bernard, Morris, Kate, Mrs. Wimbush, and Jane are all meddlers—without malice, but nevertheless flagrant meddlers in the lives of their friends. That friend who means no harm but knows not the limit to the privileges of friendship is no better than an enemy. James pilloried the type and exposed its obnoxious features in these six studies of trespassers.

III

With James's eight stories of parasites, we come closer to his theme of emotional cannibalism. These stories all contain, and chiefly deal with, people who live at the expense of others, either financially or emotionally or both. Every story, however, is told from the point of view of the host rather than from that of the parasite. What to do with this parasite is the question always being asked. It is not easily answered, because the parasite is usually a close friend, or the friend of a beloved relative, or a wife, daughter, father, or mother; and the only life he or she has consists of whatever existence he can succeed in subtracting from his host. The principal nexus of James's scrutiny, his focal interest, is the effect on the host of the existence of the parasite in his life.

Max Austin, in *A Light Man* (1869), attempts to influence the aged and wealthy Frederick Sloane to change his will so as to substitute his own name in place of Theodore Lisle's as the principal beneficiary. This project is the more dastardly in that Max's presence in Sloane's house is due to Theodore's friendly and generous act in asking Sloane to invite Max (a school chum of Theodore) for a month's stay. The old man dies, however, after the first will is destroyed and before the new one is made, and so Max not only fails to get the money for himself but also deprives his friend Theodore of the fortune that had been destined for him.

Caroline Spencer, in *Four Meetings* (1877), spends her life, as well as her frail income as a New England schoolteacher, supporting, and even acting as housekeeper to, the fake countess who, pretending to have been the wife of Caroline's deceased cousin, had come, uninvited, from France to live with her American relative-in-law. This same cousin, furthermore, had some years previously met Caroline when she landed in Europe and borrowed from her all the money she had saved from several years of teaching, so that her long-planned European tour had lasted only thirteen hours.

The Pension Beaurepas (1879) tells mainly of tolerant, patient Mr. Ruck and how he was victimized by Mrs. Ruck and Sophy Ruck, his foolish and innocently selfish spendthrift wife and daughter.

Basil Ransom, in *The Bostonians* (1885), defeats Olive Chancellor in his struggle with her for the possession of Verena Tarrant by virtue of his truer understanding of what Verena's nature, now only budding, would be like in its full flowering if the internal promise of the bud were permitted to work out its destiny unmolested. In spite of the fact that Verena lives in Olive's house and is financially beholden to Olive, Olive rather than Verena is the real parasite. Olive's expensive grooming of Verena for a public-speaking career in the interest of women's suffrage, instead of being a fostering of the personal and spiritual development of the girl, is really a warping of Verena's true nature, a sublimated and disguised lesbian feeding on Verena. Basil Ransom unwinds the constricting vine which, in the person of Olive, had entwined itself around Verena, and had forced her to grow into shapes foreign to her natural destiny. She is rescued from Olive's lust of dominion and emotional parasitism by the man who marries her.

Morgan Moreen, the precocious and distinguished little invalid in *The Pupil* (1891), is acutely, but silently, conscious of his parents' imperfections. He sees through the various strategems that his father employs to evade making an attempt to earn an honest living. The family moves frequently from one residence to another, and Morgan knows that many unpaid bills are left behind. The Moreens live above their means in order to make an impression on possible suiters for the two daughters. Morgan watches his parents plot and scheme to marry one or both of his sisters, or even his brother Ulick, to someone rich enough to support them all.

Morgan winces in secret at the shoddy parasitism, general shiftlessness, and sickening pretentiousness of his family's way of living. A succession of private tutors takes the place of school in Morgan's life, but each one leaves after a short time because Mr. Moreen neglects to pay him any wages. The last one, Pemberton, stays for several years, however, because he likes the boy so well. Morgan's parents take advantage of Pemberton's affection for their son by reducing his pay gradually to board and room only.

Morgan begins to suffer, as well as wince, when he grows older, falls in love with Pemberton, and realizes that his beloved tutor is sacrificing a great deal, including an academic career, for his sake. Although continually urged by Morgan to go away in search of the brilliant career he deserves, Pemberton is so attracted by the boy's fineness of perception and really exquisite capacities that he stays until the very end. When the family is finally evicted from its living quarters, all the mean and petty plots having come to naught,

Morgan is seized with a paroxysm of shame for his parents, as well as of excitement at the prospect of going away from them to live with Pemberton, and of fear that he will be a burdensome impediment in Pemberton's career. The throes of these combined emotions, in which his dismay at his parents' parasitical way of life has culminated, are too much for him, and the boy Morgan dies in Pemberton's arms.

Leolin Stormer, in *Greville Fane* (1893), is an evil and pretentious, cynical parasite who lives a shady man-about-town life on the earnings of his mother, an author of cheap society novels under the pseudonym of Greville Fane. Leolin deludes his mother into thinking that he will begin writing presently and take over from her the burden of earning the income on which the two of them live. His mother's novels sell in smaller and smaller editions, forcing her to work continuously harder to support herself and her son, but Leolin delays taking the pen from her hand on the pretext that he has not yet completed the researches into life that are preparing him for a writing career. This goes on year after year until finally the mother dies of exhaustion—whereupon Leolin and his sister Ethel have a sordid quarrel over the proceeds of the literary remains of Greville Fane.

Mrs. Rimmle, the crafty and tyrannical centenarian in *"Europe"* (1899), prevents her three daughters, Becky, Jane, and Maria, from having any life of their own, keeps them, unmarried and untraveled, ministering to her pretended invalidism until they are old women. She has promised them year after year, ever since they were young girls, a trip to Europe for a summer's tour, and each time has found some excuse to postpone its execution to another year. She lives on to an incredible old age, as though she were a vampire feeding on her own offspring. Finally Jane, with a desperate wrench, and against her mother's open prohibition, tears herself free from the maternal roof and sails for Europe in the company of a friendly family. When her friends return to America, Jane refuses to return with them. She establishes a permanent residence in Europe, financed by her sister Becky, who admires from afar Jane's rebellious spirit. The third sister, Maria, never rebels in any way, although she is conscious of her martyrdom. Mrs. Rimmle is a salient specimen of that type of mother who, instead of preparing them for a free and independent life of their own, emotionally enslaves and exploits her children.

Peter Brench, in *The Tree Of Knowledge* (1900), voluntarily permits the woman he loves to think that she has succeeded for an entire lifetime in making him believe something that she herself secretly knows to be false. She is the wife of Morgan Mallow, a sculptor whose productions do not sell. Morgan maintains that his work is too good to sell, and his wife pretends to believe in this palpable fiction, out of consideration for her husband's feelings. She insists also on Peter Brench's concurrence in her voiced opinion, concealing from both him and her husband her real opinion that the sculptures are worthless.

Although it is upon this pretense that she bases her sexual loyalty to Morgan in the face of Peter's love for her, Peter obeys her wish that he never question the accuracy of Morgan's self-estimate. Mrs. Mallow and Peter Brench love each other in sexual abstinence for a lifetime, both knowing, but neither one realizing that the other knows too, the falsity of the pretense upon which their abstinence is based. They never breathe their real opinion of Morgan, either to each other or to Mrs. Mallow's son Lance.

Lance, however, grew up to be an artist, and found out for himself that his father was a humbug. He challenged his mother on her opinion of his father's artistic ability, and she was finally forced to confess to him that she had been aware of the truth all her life. Lance then tells Peter, who thereby discovers for the first time that the woman he had loved for a lifetime had known as well as he that her husband was a weak imposter, protected from the bitterness of self-knowledge by the sheer generosity of his wife and the man she loves. Morgan Mallow, by virtue of his inoffensive weakness of character, had been enabled to levy tribute all his life from the people around him and so prevent them from realizing their natural destiny.

The parasites in these stories either will not or cannot stand alone; they are determined to avoid sustaining themselves, so long as they can be sustained by others. Misdirection rather than weakness accounts for their parasitism. Lack of strength or intelligence cannot be charged against Max Austin, the fake countess, Olive Chancellor, the senior Moreens, Leolin Stormer, Mrs. Rimmle, or even Morgan Mallow. They exercise abilities which are above average in making depredations on people whose sensibilities are superior to theirs.

The superiority of the host consists in his ability to imaginatively and sympathetically undergo the emotional experience which the parasite would undergo should he be rebuffed. The power to partake of another's sorrow by anticipation and then to refrain from the act which would precipitate that sorrow: this power, possessed by the host but denied to the parasite, marks the line of cleavage between the more and the less conscious man. James will permit his Caroline Spencers to sacrifice everything else in their lives, bit by bit, but never their greatest possession— the power to sense another's feelings.

IV

The parasite uses peaceful means to accomplish his ends. He works on the sympathies of his victims and makes a pretense of conferring some equivalent in exchange for his spongings. The coercer, however, takes one step closer to open war and makes forcible use of some advantage he possesses over the person he preys upon. In each of James's six stories of coercion, the advantage derives from the authority of a position rather than from the weight of personal merit. The coercer is always a parent or a guardian or a wife to whom subordination is due because of his or her status. The coercive exercise of arbitrary authority in opposition to the needs of the governed is, therefore, the object of James's censure in these stories.

In *Master Eustace* (1871), a violence done to a girl by her parents brings in its train another violence done to her son by the girl, now a parent in her turn, and the final outcome is of course tragic. The girl's parents had forced her to marry another man instead of her lover, by whom she was with child at the time. Her husband having died shortly after the marriage, and her lover having gone to Australia and married another woman, she overidolizes her son Eustace—the image of his father and her only emotional resource—to a degree that amounts to emotional exploitation. Eustace grows to manhood so emotionally dependent on his mother that when his real father (of whose existence Eustace had never been aware) returns a widower from Australia and marries the girl he had loved in his youth, Eustace turns with bitter savagery on his mother, accusing her of faithlessness to *him*, her own son. She dies of the shock.

In *Roderick Hudson* (1875), the coercion of Christina Light into marriage with Prince Casamassima shatters Roderick's power as a creative artist and frustrates Rowland Mallet's project of assisting Roderick's embryonic genius to grow to full maturity. If Roderick's emotional relation with Christina had been permitted to run its natural course without interference on the part of her parents, Mrs. Light and the Cavaliere Giacosa, Roderick would have been able to ride through the emotional rapids which Christina had occasioned in his life, and he would have lived to become the great sculptor of which his first few productions contained the promise.

Urbain de Bellegarde, with the help of his mother, Madame de Bellegarde, in *The American* (1876), coerces his sister Claire de Cintre into breaking off her engagement to marry Christopher Newman, and they thus do incalculable evil by determining the course of other people's lives without consulting the deepest needs of the people coerced. Since both

Christopher and Claire had seemed peculiarly fitted to comprehend the other's qualities and to find in them the complement of their own, their failure to marry was especially tragic. Claire becomes a Carmelite nun, utterly lost to the man for whom she would have made a superb wife.

Lord Edmund Tester, in *The Path Of Duty* (1884), inflicted a lifelong injury on three people by his insistence that his son Ambrose acquire a wife while his father was still alive. Up to now Ambrose had remained unmarried because the woman he loved, Margaret Vandeleur, had a husband. Obeying his father's command, he courted and proposed marriage to Joscelind Bernardstone, a young girl who fell deeply in love with him. Shortly before the marriage, Margaret was freed by the unexpected death of her husband, but it was too late for Ambrose to avoid marrying Joscelind. Ambrose and Margaret continue their sexless friendship, and Joscelind bears Ambrose's children, half knowing that Ambrose's love is elsewhere owned. No one of the three enjoys the complete life that might have been possible, had it not been for the father's unwarranted interference in the life of his son.

Raymond Benyon, in *Georgina's Reasons* (1885), permits his wife, Georgina, to wheedle from him during their honeymoon a promise to keep their marriage a secret until she withdraws the prohibition. Her parents having expressed opposition to Raymond as her suitor, she wants to delay as long as possible their discovery of her marriage to him. This weakness of his, and the unfair advantage which she took of him, starts a chain of events which, several years later, block his marriage to Kate Theory. Raymond is a lieutenant in the navy, and shortly after his marriage to Georgina he is ordered to sea. When Georgina finds herself pregnant, she persuades a friend of her mother to take her to Italy, so that her parents will not learn of her marriage. She gives the baby to an Italian family without ever telling Raymond that he is a father. The woman who had taken Georgina to Italy, however, writes to Raymond and tells him what Georgina has done. Raymond tries to find the baby and fails, whereupon he and Georgina quarrel and stop corresponding. Ten years later, having fallen in love with Kate Theory, he wants to divorce Georgina in order to marry Kate. He finds Georgina and learns that she has married again without bothering to get a divorce. She now refuses to divorce Raymond because that would reveal her first marriage to her second husband. Raymond cannot break his promise never to reveal his marriage to her, and he cannot marry Kate while he has another wife; so he is forced to settle down and wait for Georgina to die.

Julia Bream, in *The Other House* (1896), by taking an unfair advantage over her husband Tony and wringing from him the deathbed promise never to marry a second wife so long as her daughter Effie was alive, started a chain of events which culminated in her daughter's murder, in her best friend (Rose Armiger) becoming a murderess, and in the tormenting and twisting of the lives of several other people. The unhappy life she had led as a stepdaughter made Julia determine that her little girl Effie would not in her turn suffer the tyrannies of a stepmother, but she overreached her warrant when, resorting to a deathbed vow, she coerced the lives which her husband and others would live after her death into channels of her own choosing.

In each of these stories, without exception, it is an innocent third person, rather than the coercer or the coerced, that suffers the greatest injury. James apparently felt that an act of coercion contained seeds of mystic evil, since he invariably traces a long train of evil consequences back to one original act of coercion. Eustace is a neurotic wreck because his grandparents interfered in their daughter's love life. Roderick's life and career are brought to an early end because the indigent Giacosa forced his daughter Christina to marry the wealthy Casamassima. Christopher carries a tomb in his heart because Urbain commanded Claire to cancel her wedding plans. Joscelind and Margaret live half lives because Lord Tester forced his son Ambrose into an immediate marriage. Kate Theory cannot fulfill her life with Raymond because Georgina had demanded an inexcusable vow from Raymond before agreeing to marry him. Tony loses his daughter Effie by murder because his wife Julia, on her deathbed, had made him promise never to give Effie a stepmother. The traumatic aftereffects of an act of violence, James says, live on long after the perpetrator has passed away.

V

The gradual crescendo in the preceding groups of stories has grown from the violence of opinion to overt meddling to parasitism to coercion, and we have now arrived at those stories which deal with the most flagrant kind of emotional cannibalism: exploitation. James wrote eight stories, three of them novels, about people who live, or at least attempt to live, emotionally or financially, on the backs of other people. Some of them practice on the credulity of others and despoil them by strategem or by fraud; others plunder and pillage under the cover of pretended affection. Deception is practiced sometimes to gain material riches and sometimes for the pleasure of exercising a despotic power over another human being. To make a dupe of one we have befriended and strip him of his money or his emotions or to make of him an involuntary means to our own ends is sheer vandalism—and James reveals a great deal of human conduct to be reducible to this term. James's central thought in this theme is that many exploiters are but dimly aware of the fact that their deeds really partake of this reprehensible nature. It is easy to recognize the vandalism of the invading Goth, the iniquity of slavery, the exploitation of poor worker by rich employer, or the crime of the embezzler, but we are not so quick to see the qualitative identity of that kind of conduct with its counterpart in our own civilized and polite patterns of behavior. What James was getting at in these stories was an accurate definition of two radically differing ways of using other people in our lives.

Sam Scrope, the young, scientific archeologist in *Adina* (1874), is severely punished for the scant respect he has shown for the historic charm of Italy and for the contempt and scorn in which he holds the Roman peasantry. The peasant youth Angelo Beati, incensed at being for a small sum so unfeelingly tricked out of his trinket which proves to be a topaz bearing the insignia of the Emperor Tiberius, discovers that Scrope is in love with a girl named Adina, whom he prizes highly. Angelo in some mysterious way wins Adina away from Scrope, elopes with and marries her; whereupon Scrope takes his invaluable topaz to the bridge of St. Angelo and drops it into the Tiber.

Anastasia Blumenthal, in *Eugene Pickering* (1874), a sophisticated, worldly woman of jaded sensibilities, charming of manner, intelligent, experienced, but false and heartless, deliberately fascinates and elicits a proposal of marriage from Eugene, who is a naive, inexperienced, and ingenuous boy. With her experienced hands she easily makes him squeak forth, like a doll, any words she wishes for. The next day after accepting his proposal of marriage, she sadistically jilts him, coolly telling him that she had merely been carrying on for her own amusement an experiment in subjugation. She is a writer and had simply fleeced him of his emotions in order to observe his behavior for use in her fiction. Eugene is harrowed and hardened by this treatment but not embittered; he has arrived at moral manhood, while Anastasia, though apparently unscathed, is doomed, the reader feels, to moral solitude.

In *The Europeans* (1878), James contrasts the dispositions of a brother and sister, Baroness Eugenia Munster and Felix Young. Eugenia, being of a predatory nature, looks only for those qualities in people which can be turned to her own advantage; while Felix, on the other hand, tries to elicit from his acquaintances a more complete expression of their native qualities than they are in the habit of furnishing. By permitting Felix to succeed in his difficult venture while meting out failure to Eugenia in her easier one, James reveals his conception of the proper and of the improper use to make of other human beings.

Isabel Archer, in *The Portrait Of A Lady* (1880), is exploited by Gilbert Osmond and Madame Merle while she is cherished, and her interests fostered, by Ralph Touchett. Ralph persuaded his father to enrich Isabel in his will so that she would have the means with which to live that life she possessed the rich, imaginative capacity to create for herself, while Gilbert could find nothing better to do with her than to despoil her not only of her fortune but of her freedom to give rein to her ability to live generously. Madame Merle and Gilbert bent and warped her to their own uses, cramped her life and made it thin. Madame Merle did it to gain a dowry for her (and Gilbert's) daughter, and Gilbert did it to get the wherewithal to browbeat the world into acceding to his good opinion of himself. Gilbert Osmond and Madame Merle are villains because they gain their ends at the expense of Isabel Archer, while Ralph Touchett is admirable because he gained his ends (or at least tried to) by aiding other people to gain theirs.

The governess, in *The Turn Of The Screw* (1898), subjects Flora and Miles, the nine- and ten-year old girl and boy who have been delivered into her power, to all the vagaries of her progressively more and more deranged mind, until through sheer terror Flora goes into a delirium with brain fever, and Miles, harder pressed than Flora, is literally scared to death.

This harrowing story of the obsessive and rapacious emotional devouring of two innocent children by an emotionally
avid governess is intensified by the tenderness with which
the two children, vaguely realizing the pathological nature
of their governess's malady, parry and avoid taking issue
with their persecutor's mania. Under the guise of a jealous
and clutching love for the children who she imagines are
being lured away from her by the evil ghosts of their previous
tutors, Peter Quint and Miss Jessel, the mad governess is
really engulfing them into the vortex of her hallucinatory
world. Their resistance first takes the form of tenderly over-
looking, pretending not to notice, the governess's peculiarities,
then of a compassionate but worried attempt to amuse her
and keep her occupied in proudly admiring the scholastic
accomplishments which she has taught them, and finally,
when their uneasiness at her excesses turns into acute fright,
of merely searching for ways of avoiding her. They never try
to fight back at her, and this is the source of the pathos in
the narrative. Flora and Miles are in the end swept away to
destruction by the force of their governess's emotional
cannibalism, of which this is the most extreme and excruciating case in James's fiction.

Merton Densher, the central character in *The Wings Of
The Dove* (1902), permits himself to be persuaded by his
fiancée, Kate Croy, to commit the evil deed of making love
to the wealthy but dying Milly Theale in order to inherit
her fortune and thereby provide the means on which they
(Kate and Merton) may marry and live after Milly's death.
Milly's discovery of their plot furnishes the deathblow to

her will to live, but she nevertheless sadly wills to Merton a large part of her fortune. Remorse then overtakes Merton and he achieves a final great victory over himself—and thereby rights himself to a degree—by refusing to accept the financial bequest and by refusing to marry Kate.

Merton Densher and Kate Croy, though both are in love, lose each other because they yield to the temptation to interfere in the life of and to make a base use of their friend Milly Theale, for their own selfish benefit and profit. Maud Lowder, Kate's aunt, is the remote cause of Kate's temptation, Merton's misdeed and trial, and Milly's saddened and hastened death, by reason of her earlier interference in Kate's plans to marry Merton. By opposing Kate's proposed marriage to Merton on the grounds of his poverty, Maud unintentionally stimulated that desire in Kate for power and position which could not resist the temptation to plunder these things from an emotionally exploited Milly.

Alice Dundene, in *The Special Type* (1903), is made use of and then discarded, without, however, suffering from resentment or any sense of humiliation. She loves her exploiter to the extent of wanting him to have what he wants, even though it is marriage to another woman.

Frank Brivet intends to provoke his wife into divorcing him so that he can marry Rose Cavenham, but he also wishes to guard Rose against the disgrace of being named as corespondent in a divorce action. So he goes about very publicly with Alice Dundene, showering attentions on her as though she were his mistress. This procedure succeeds in inciting Mrs. Brivet to divorce him, naming Alice as corespondent. Brivet then marries Rose Cavenham, who has connived with him in using Alice Dundene as a decoy to receive the embarrassing publicity of the divorce court. Rose benefits by being shielded from scandal and by getting Brivet for her husband, while Alice's reputation bears the expense.

Alice Dundene stands for those exploited ones who, by their capacity for unacquisitive feeling, morally triumph over their exploiters.

The Velvet Glove (1909) tells of a man's disappointment at finding that a woman was gracious to him not for himself alone, as he had thought, but for a service that it was in his power to do her. John Berridge was a famous writer who was asked by Amy Evans to contribute a Preface to her novel. When he met her that evening at the party in Gloriani's studio, he had thought that she was a transcendently beautiful woman, a Princess, a work of art in her own right, but before the evening was over she turned out to be a writer of novels, and poor novels at that, under the pseudonym of Amy Evans. She had treated him with such lovely graciousness and had talked so fluently of her artistic sympathy with him as he was revealed in his books that he thought of her as an Olympian goddess who had deigned to fall in love with him, preferring him—a young writer just become famous—to the great Sculptor and to the great Dramatist who were also present at the party. In appearance she was Romance itself, but in reality she was only an amateurish scribbler about Romance, and one who did not scruple to use her romance-inspiring self as a bait for a favor to the fifth-rate writer she was.

This story is not only an attack on women who look and act and dress as though they were made for love and love alone, and then offer, not love, but its simulacrum to gain an ulterior end: it is also a fable about appearance and reality, in which, contrary to many of James's stories, reality comes off second best. By making an illegitimate use of her superb appearance to gain an advantage for her common-place reality, Amy Evans exploited herself. John Berridge loves the Princess, but he snubs Amy Evans by refusing to write her Preface.

Of these eight stories of exploitation, *The Turn Of The Screw* is the most abstract and formalized. The governess's only motive is the satisfaction of her emotional need, which is pathological only in its intensity. The basic theme of *The Turn Of The Screw*—emotional exploitation—is identical with that of *The Wings Of The Dove* and *The Portrait Of A Lady*. The sense of horror we get from *The Turn Of The Screw* comes from its purity; we cannot say of the governess as we can of Madame Merle or Kate Croy: she wanted money. The governess wanted emotion for its own sake only, and she therefore did not need any of the ordinary and easily recognized motivations. She is a symbol of that rapacity which peoples its private world with emotions torn from their context and filched from the persons of those whom it has victimized.

VI

Three stories of revenge, that most frenzied form of emotional cannibalism, bring to an end James's account of man's misuse of his fellow men. That revenge is folly and its sweetness fleeting everybody knows but nobody heeds. And the reason for this James wrote these stories to discover.

The story *Guest's Confession* (1872) tells of the evil consequences of an act of humiliation inflicted by the righteous but malevolent Edgar Musgrave on the more weak than wicked John Guest. The humiliation of Guest occurred in the presence of Edgar's cousin David, who was engaged to marry Guest's daughter Laura, and Guest promptly conceived a hatred of David because the sight of him, innocent bystander though he was, served to remind Guest of the degradation he had suffered. Laura and David love each other, but John Guest, maddened by David's association with the scene of violence and shame, refuses them permission to marry. After a bitter struggle, David finally succeeds in overcoming Laura's father's aversion to him as a son-in-law, but Edgar Musgrave's inhumanity to John Guest had seared an indelible black mark on the innocent and guilty alike. We pity Guest, and are patient with him in his reluctance to permit the marriage, because Musgrave had pressed an advantage to an inordinate degree.

Professor Fargo, in the story of that name (1874), is a fake spiritualist and clairvoyant who forms a partnership with a needy mathematical genius, Col. Gifford, and his daughter. The three of them constitute a traveling troupe. Col. Gifford, a true scientist, despises Professor Fargo the charlatan and in an exasperated moment rashly challenges Fargo's much-touted spiel on "spiritual magnetism." Fargo triumphs in the end and gets his revenge by first secretly practicing hypnotism on the Colonel's deaf-mute daughter, then goading the Colonel into dissolving the partnership, and finally by hypnotizing the girl into staying with him instead of going away with her father. This breaks the Colonel's heart; he loses his mind and spends the remainder of his life in an asylum.

May Grantham, in *The Two Faces* (1901), succumbs to the temptation to take a dishonorable advantage of her opportunity to wreak social ruin on Valda, her successful rival for wifehood to Lord Gwyther. After he had roused, by spending so much time in her company, May Grantham's expectation of being asked to become Lady Gwyther, Lord Gwyther astounded her and her friends by announcing his marriage in Germany to a very young girl, daughter of a noble family there. He then brings her to May Grantham and asks May to take charge of dressing the girl properly for her debut at a great and formal social gathering in England. May accepts the charge, with seeming graciousness takes custody of the girl, and then carefully plans her malevolent revenge. She lets no one catch sight of Valda from that day until all the guests are assembled at the great party. Then Valda enters. May Grantham had dressed her with an atrocity of art, had "overloaded her like a monkey in a show." Her face is scared and sick, and it is apparent that she will never be able to undo this first detrimental impression that May had so diabolically contrived to effect. May's face, on the other hand, possesses a hard, resplendent beauty: it is her delicious moment of triumphant revenge.

These three stories of revenge describe the final stages in that path of conduct which began with the stories of opinion.

The aggressive person who is too ready to form opinions about his neighbors has taken the road on which, farther on, travels the type of man who knows only one answer to an affront: retaliation. The reason revenge is so often resorted to in spite of its universally acknowledged folly is that the need for revenge is a required consistent outcome of conduct of which the folly is not immediately visible. Failure to refrain from passing judgment on a neighbor's conduct ultimately deprives one of the capacity to forego an act of revenge, just as an infinitesimal deflection from a direct course will in time bring one to a position of wide divergence from the norm.

———

The conclusion inherent in James's stories of emotional cannibalism is that inevitable defeat lies in wait for him who seeks to procure from other people that strength which can only come from within. The thought residue common to all forty stories in this group is an assertion concerning the viciousness of any substitute for inner reliance. The substitute in most widespread use, according to James, consists of a distortion of human beings other than ourselves into mere functions of our emotions. To make this use of other people is to consume them, and both the user and the used, the consumer and the consumed, are depleted by it.

Chapter Two

CONSIDERATION FOR OTHERS

THE CONSTRUCTIVE CORRELATIVE to James's theme of emotional cannibalism constitutes the informing principle of another major portion of James's fiction. In his countertheme, James proposes to show that the alternative to self-defeating depredations on others is not disregard of their existence but an attentiveness to it differently motivated. The existence of other people in our lives can be a boon instead of a pitfall, notwithstanding the overwhelming frequency with which people do prove to be pitfalls to one another.

Failure to venerate the emotional autonomy of another person makes him our pitfall and hurts both him and us, while self-possession—not only the other person's but our own as well—is enhanced by an active effort to discover and satisfy the other's real wants. To the emotional cannibal stands opposed that person who realizes that all other people are his alter egos. In James's second large group of stories the type character accumulates consciousness—the only real wealth—by investigating and reflecting upon and profoundly respecting the sensibilities of others. Personal relations comprise, in James's fiction, not only the field in which character is exposed but, far more, that in which it is gained or lost. The kind of use to which we put those we know determines whether the fund of consciousness with which we begin life shall dwindle or grow, and James's stories of consideration for others show how growth of consciousness takes place.

I

In two of James's stories, a sudden increase of awareness comes to the leading figures through the agency of an unexpected insight into the vanity of revenge. Of all the forms of emotional cannibalism, revenge alone carries within it the seeds of its own cure. It is not so easy to delude oneself as to the true nature and basic motive of revenge as it is to find some plausible sanction for opinionatedness, meddling, parasitism, coercion, and exploitation. Revenge, the violent extreme, has torn off its disguises and, if the person who harbors it takes a second look, he may recognize it for what it is: futile self-aggrandizement in the mask of justice.

Christopher Newman, in *The American* (1876), decides not to take advantage of his opportunity for revenge on the Bellegardes who had so cruelly blocked his marriage to Claire de Cintre. He had discovered the secret Bellegarde family crime, the publishing abroad of which by him would bring scandal and disgrace upon the proud authors of his grief. Christopher's decision to spare them was due to his undefined but genuine feeling that consideration for them on his part would be more subtly galling to them, in its evident superiority over their inconsiderate conduct towards him, than any obviously revengeful deed.

Mrs. Warren Hope, in *The Abasement Of The Northmores* (1900), finds unexpected and intensely welcome confirmation in the exposed vacuousness and totally undistinguished character of Lord Northmore's letters, which were published shortly after his death, of her lifelong belief that her unsuccessful husband, Warren Hope, whom she had preferred to John Northmore when they had in their youth both courted her, was immeasurably superior in ability to the conspicuously successful Lord Northmore. During her entire life it had galled her that the British political public had acclaimed and made a national figure of John Northmore, while her husband, Warren Hope, had lived and died unknown to fame. Now, with the publication of the Northmore letters, all the world can see how shallow a mind had written them. Mrs. Hope determines to publish her husband's marvelous letters, which reveal an ability of so much greater scope. But first she visits Lady Northmore, in order to exult, to see the once proud lady humbled by the world's belated scorn of the bloated Northmore. She finds the great Northmores, mother and daughters, so consciously weak and flat, however, that she has not the heart to exult or even to publish her own husband's letters so soon as to invite invidious comparison with Northmore's. Out of pity for Lady Northmore, after a lifetime of acidulous envy, she postpones until after her own death the publication of Warren's letters.

The prime significance of these two stories lies in the enlightenment of Christopher Newman and Mrs. Hope, their translation to a new and superior level of awareness. They find themselves suddenly unwilling to exercise the vengeance which for so long had seemed so very desirable. The imminence of their opponents' downfall enabled them to foresee imaginatively in greater detail than before the humiliating spectacle of a human being tumbled in the dust—and their latent humanity recoiled from the vision. A new strength had come to them, a strength to let people have even what they had unjustly acquired.

II

The reward of enlightenment accrues to another group of James's characters as a result of observing the consequences of their own past behavior. In every instance, it is an act of intervention in the life of another which, by having borne bitter fruit, leads to self-examination, rue, repentance, and graduation to a higher degree of awareness. These people do not belong to that higher order of being which proves in the crucible of experience to be fine-grained; they merely possess the merit of having eventually become aware of their own coarseness and of doing then what they can to alleviate the evil effects of their former deeds. By costly trial and error they have learned the merit of some measure of sensibility; and we know, when we finish James's account of this crucial segment of their lives, that their subsequent life will differ from their earlier principally in the degree to which consideration for others is practiced therein.

Henry Wilmerding, in *The Solution* (1889), is the target of so cruel and heartless a practical joke that he is almost precipitated into marriage with an especially obnoxious girl with whom he is not in love. While attending a picnic as a guest during the early days of his first visit to Italy, he, an American, had taken a fifteen-minute stroll with one of the English girl guests, Veronica Goldie, into the solitude of a grove adjacent to the picnic grounds, from which none of the other guests had strayed. A few days later, two of his friends in the diplomatic corps, after carefully planning their plot so as to take advantage of Wilmerding's ignorance of the customs of the country, have little trouble in persuading him that, since public notice had been taken of his absence with the unchaperoned girl during the stroll, he had compromised her in the eyes of everybody present at the picnic. They tell him that when a man of honor compromises a girl, his behavior is considered tantamount to a proposal of marriage.

Wilmerding suffers to think that he had done the poor girl a wrong and promptly asks her to marry him. When she accepts, one of the practical jokers repents of having so viciously meddled in Wilmerding's life and in desperation begs the woman he is engaged to marry, a Mrs. Rushbrook, to do something to rescue Wilmerding from his predicament. She does so—by marrying him herself.

Louisa Pallant, in the story of that name (1888), retrieves in some degree the loss of moral stature which, by jilting, and thereby injuring, a poorer man in order to marry a richer one, she now, twenty years later, realizes she had inflicted on herself. Louisa's self-knowledge and consequent self-censure is quickened by her seeing, in her hard-natured and ambitious daughter Linda, what she herself must have been like when she was Linda's age. Upon observing that Linda is about to trap in marriage, for his money, the nephew of the man whom Louisa had jilted because of his lack of money, Louisa takes it upon herself to warn the young man and to rescue him from her daughter Linda's acquisitive and exploiting designs. In this way Louisa does penance and symbolic reparation for the injury to her early lover which lay heavy on her conscience.

Adela Chart, in *The Marriages* (1891), lived to repent bitterly for the act of intervention by which she prevented the marriage of her father to Mrs. Churchley. Fiercely believing that her father's approaching second marriage would be a gross disloyalty to her dead mother, Adela took the step of calling on Mrs. Churchley and telling her lies about the abuses which the first Mrs. Chart had suffered from her husband, hoping that Mrs. Churchley would thereby be dissuaded from becoming the second Mrs. Chart. Later Adela learns not only that she has hurt her father very deeply but that she has also injured her adored brother Godfrey, for the annulment of whose secret marriage to a vicious woman, public knowledge of which would wreck his career in the diplomatic service, the wealthy Mrs. Churchley had promised to furnish the funds as soon as she became his stepmother. Adela tries to repair the damage she has done by calling on Mrs. Churchley again and retracting the lies she has told, but she is too late. Mrs. Churchley has already become engaged to marry someone else. She also informs Adela that she had not believed the lies but that she had offered to marry Mr. Chart if he would not insist that she live in the same house with Adela, whereupon Adela's father had himself broken off the engagement. Adela knows too that he has impoverished himself by buying off Godfrey's wife. In anguish Adela realizes that a lifetime of devotion to her father will not make amends for the emotional and financial distress she has inflicted on him by not minding her own business.

Mrs. Marden, in *Sir Edmund Orme* (1892), had in her youth jilted a man, causing him to commit suicide. She recovered so little from this blow to her conscience that, when her daughter Charlotte began in her turn to be courted by suitors, Mrs. Marden's terror that her daughter might also turn out to be a jilt causes her to see the ghost of Sir Edmund Orme, her own dead lover, come into the room whenever a man who is in love with Charlotte is present. The ghost is finally exorcized when Charlotte accepts in marriage the first man who proposes to her.

Mark Monteith, in *A Round Of Visits* (1910), unwittingly ignites the sense of remorse and self-judgment which governs the last few hours of the life of his friend Newton Winch, an embezzler and a suicide. Phil Bloodgood, another of Mark's friends, had just absconded with Mark's and several other persons' money. Mark's state of mind is not that of shock or rage at having lost his money but that of grief for his friend Phil. He can hardly bear to think how Phil must feel, knowing himself to be guilty of such a breach of fidelity. He wants to find Phil and comfort him in his distress, but Phil has disappeared. Mark visits several people who have been mutual friends of him and Phil, but the only one who listens sympathetically and seems to understand Mark's attitude of compassion for the man who had robbed him is Newton Winch. Mark does not know until later that Newton's position is identical with Phil's, that everything that he is saying about Phil can also be said about Newton, or that, while he talks, the motive for the suicide that Newton is about to commit is changing from fear of the law to remorse and self-judgment.

These five stories of remorse reach down to the roots of the conceptual error which gave birth to the regretted deeds. From the practical joker to the embezzler, all of these finally remorseful people realize that their usage of other people has maimed themselves. Tragedy, however, is not the keynote of their histories. The fundamental fact salvaged from these ruins, the characteristic Jamesian trophy, shines forth in the transformed consciousnesses of the repentant. They have been blindfolded, and now they see. In their limited way, they too adumbrate the most conscious man.

III

A superior rank in James's hierarchy of conscious characters consists of persons who, however hard pressed, succeed in maintaining a scrupulous respect for the rights and feelings of people foreign in kind to themselves. The crucible of experience proves them sound, although in the burning which tests their mettle they do not escape anguish. Their virtues are admirable but not supernal. The four stories which James devotes to them bridge the chasm between his stories of emotional cannibalism and his stories of compassion. Standing as they do midway between his two major themes, they define the issue and present the alternatives perhaps more clearly than does any other group of James's productions.

George Littlemore, in *The Siege Of London* (1883), governs the conduct of his life with principal reference to one cardinal, self-imposed rule: that of complete nonintervention in the lives of other people. Not only by conscious reasoning on the logic of conduct but also, perhaps mainly, by the characteristic bent of his nature, Littlemore habitually holds himself scrupulously aloof from any act which might, however slightly, affect the course of any other human being's life. He attempts at all times to remain the pure observer, neither helping nor hindering, neither fostering nor frustrating the purposes and endeavors of other people. It seems to be an intuition and a conviction of his that for him to tip the scales by any exertion of personal influence so as to affect the course of events would be a violation of his code of honor as an observer of life—as dishonest for him as it would be for a research scientist to allow any personal predilection of his to predetermine by interference with the data and laws of induction the final conclusion of a scientific investigation.

The story tells of one incident which severely tests his power to maintain the inviolability of his chosen role. For at least once in his life he is almost backed into a corner and forced to decide a woman's fate, as well as that of several other persons whose lives are involved with hers. Circumstances have placed him at the crux of several convergent and clashing lines of pressure, and only the utmost wariness on his part and a bit of audacious ingenuity on the part of the woman save him from touching, and thereby deflecting, the course of events.

Nancy Beck, whom Littlemore had known in Arizona and whom he does not think respectable, had subsequently married a Mr. Headway and on his death inherited his fortune. She appears in London in the company of Sir Arthur Desmesne, who apparently is on the verge of asking her to become Lady Desmesne. This will be a great and much-to-

be-desired victory for Nancy Headway, who had been decisively snubbed by New York society women, but Sir
Arthur's mother, who is a close friend of Littlemore's sister,
Mrs. Dolphin, deeply distrusts Mrs. Headway and definitely
does not want her as a daughter-in-law. She enlists Mrs.
Dolphin's active support in her effort to dissuade Sir Arthur
from the disastrous marriage, and Littlemore's sister demands
of her brother that he state his opinion, in quarters accessible
to Sir Arthur, that Mrs. Headway is not respectable. Mrs.
Headway also approaches Littlemore and asks him, as an
old friend, to discreetly assist her in eliciting from Sir Arthur
a definite proposal of marriage. Littlemore refuses to do
either one thing or the other, and, although the pressure from
both sides gets very intense, he does not obey the impulse
to run away. He holds his ground and tells both claimants
that it is none of his business whom Sir Arthur marries.
Mrs. Headway at last artfully forces the issue by asking
Littlemore, in Sir Arthur's presence, to tell her suitor whether
or not she is respectable. Sir Arthur then, of course, denies
that he requires Littlemore's opinion on that score, and on
the following day the Desmesne-Headway engagement is
publicly announced.

Francie Dosson, in *The Reverberator* (1888), spurns George
Flack's offer of marriage because she understands the
crudity of his failure to be ashamed of having hurt the feelings of people whose sensitiveness neither he nor she, for
that matter, could comprehend. Gaston Probert deliberately
chooses to marry Francie, in the face of his family's prohibition, because he sees that Francie's delicacy of feeling, in

spite of appearances, is superior to that of his own people. After consenting to Gaston's engagement to marry Francie, the Proberts are humiliated and infuriated by reading in an American newspaper an account of their private and not entirely creditable family history, which Francie had at one time innocently related to her friend George Flack, an American journalist, in return for various friendly services. Francie, summoned to a meeting of the assembled family, receives their horrified excommunication. This event precipitates in both Francie and Gaston a fierce and concentrated course of education in values, from which both emerge victorious—Francie over the common human impulse to explain and defend an innocent misdeed, to fight back, and Gaston over the lifelong-inculcated family training which threatened to obscure his perception of the true nature of Francie's conduct. These two young people grow before our very eyes from innocent and unquestioning products of their respective environments into mature persons knowing the grounds on which they make their decisions. They have become free moral agents, respecting each other's and other people's feelings as real entities.

Ruth Anvoy, in *The Coxon Fund* (1894), faces an extremely difficult decision, and emerges from her trial victorious, but shorn of the husband and the fortune that it had been in her power to secure. The bestowal of a substantial trust fund on some genius whose poverty prevents the exercise of his talent has been delegated to her by an aunt, Lady Coxon, in a will which also stipulates Ruth's right to retain the money for her own uses should she fail to find a man who fits the specifications of the bequest. Ruth's problem is aggravated by the fact that when Lady Coxon dies Ruth is a rich heiress but that by the time the will is read Ruth is a penniless girl, her father having suddenly lost his fortune and died. Her fiancé, George Gravener, is a brilliant but impecunious young member of Parliament who had been depending on Ruth's money to further his political career. Now that her father has died moneyless, George wants her to keep the Coxon fund, become Mrs. Gravener, and consider her husband to be the needy genius—albeit a political one—for whom the bequest was destined.

Ruth Anvoy, however, knows Frank Saltram. Many people, and Ruth among them, have never known any other man to possess Frank Saltram's great power to open their eyes to new intellectual vistas, to lift them to new intellectual planes on which they would then remain the rest of their lives. The pity of it is, in his friends' opinion, that he has done this only by occasional inspired talk, and in private homes. He is a genius of a talker, but he has neither lectured nor written. Moreover, Saltram is a drunkard and a sponger. He supports neither himself nor his wife and children; his friends pay all his bills. Ruth thinks that perhaps Saltram would give up drinking and sponging and begin to realize his genius in print or on the lecture platform if he should become financially independent, the legal recipient of the income from the Coxon fund. To her mind, Frank Saltram fits the specifications of the bequest.

She finally makes her decision; she names Saltram beneficiary of the Coxon fund, knowing that by so doing she not only loses George Gravener but also impoverishes herself. She triumphs over the temptation to take personal—though legal—advantage, even in her dire need, of a trust. Saltram does not perform as she had anticipated: upon receiving the money he promptly gets saturated with alcohol and soon dies. But that does not invalidate Ruth's decision, because the money, in Ruth's opinion, rightfully belonged to Saltram, the man who, as a needy genius, met the requirements named in the Coxon will.

Fleda Vetch, in *The Spoils Of Poynton* (1897), in much the same way as Ruth Anvoy of the previous story, emerges victorious from an extremely severe trial of temptation, at the price of the man she loves and of worldly wealth. Fleda is a companion to Mrs. Gereth, to whose son Owen, whom Fleda loves, had been willed by Mr. Gereth, the deceased father, the great house of Poynton and all of the priceless antique furniture which Mrs. Gereth had collected throughout a lifetime of arduous but loving expenditure of money and taste. Owen is also in love with Fleda, but before meeting Fleda he had become prematurely engaged to Mona Brigstock, a coarse and vicious girl who has no sensitiveness for the exquisite furniture at Poynton.

Mrs. Gereth wants Fleda to take Owen away from Mona and marry him herself. This Fleda could do, not only because she and Owen are in love, but also because she knows that Owen is held to his engagement to marry Mona not by emotional attachment but by his sense of obligation, as would be expected of a man who has given his word. He has almost, though inarticulately, begged Fleda to find some way to extricate him from his engagement to Mona, and his nearly mute appeal is ably seconded by his mother who uses both the most excruciating pressure and the most softening emotional bribery to persuade Fleda to capture Owen. Fleda is beset not only from these two quarters but also from within, for her own almost abject love for Owen unsettles, weakens, and finally exhausts her resistance to the project. Finally unnerved, Fleda telegraphs Owen, asking him to come to her—but it is too late; he is already married.

Why did she resist? Because she believed that any one who lifts a finger for his own benefit at the expense of someone else's rightful claim just to that degree defeats himself—and deprives himself of the status of free moral agent. For one's own sake one must defend the title of even the poorest creature in the world to consideration of his rightful claim. Fleda would accept Owen only if Mona by her own free and voluntary act would release him from his promise to marry her.

Fleda is not unhappy at losing Owen; she maintains her happiness by not surrendering to the temptation to reach out a grasping hand for him. The exercise of the acquisitive desire at the expense of the feelings of another is what Fleda feared and avoided—and in so doing she is one of the rarest of successes.

These four persons—Fleda Vetch, Ruth Anvoy, Francie Dosson, George Littlemore—were pressed by circumstances, by their friends, and by strong motives of their own to offend persons with whom they were themselves not sympathetic; but they resolutely refused to do so. They would neither encroach on the rights nor offend the sensibilities of another person, even though that person were their inferior and even though refusal to so encroach and offend deprived themselves and persons they loved of great benefits. George Littlemore would not hurt Mrs. Headway, whom he did not admire, even to please his sister. Francie Dosson would not hurt the Proberts, whom she did not understand and who had hurt her, even to clear herself of a false and cruel accusation. Ruth Anvoy would not deprive Frank Saltram, whom she knew to be a shiftless and weak character, of the Coxon fund income, even to provide herself with the wherewithal on which to live or to retain her lover. Fleda Vetch would not dispossess Mona Brigstock, whom she despised, of her fiance, even to protect her benefactress, Mrs. Gereth, from the loss of Poynton or to secure in marriage the man she loved.

By endowing these four characters with the strength to refrain, at whatever cost, from trespassing on the self-possession of any other human being, however despicable, James directs our attention to the excellences of a virtue which he finds to be too rare in mankind.

IV

Ideal characters are just as real as faulty ones. Otherwise every character would be either a dupe or a rogue. James was one writer who had the courage to say what he knew to be true: that there are people in the world who are not rogues or dupes. To the discomfiture of those who pride themselves on being "tough-minded" and who are thereby gulled into confusing the ideal with the romantic, James possessed the vital strength to place in some of his stories characters who are quixotic only to the matter-of-fact, visionary only to the ignoble, and ethereal only to the inverted romantics. Renunciation is all very well, but it is only one of the forms of nobility. To place the emphasis upon the thing renounced instead of upon the thing chosen signifies failure to fully comprehend the real superiority of a superior value. James's stories of affirmation succeed in placing the emphasis where it belongs—which is decidedly not the same thing as "eating your cake and having it too."

One of James's earliest and slightest stories foreshadows faintly the positives of conduct which he was later to formulate in a maturer art. *At Isella* (1871), in which the narrator assists a chance acquaintance, a young married lady who had been an unhappy wife for five years, to continue her flight from her husband and towards the lover whom she wishes to join, indicates James's sympathy with the forces of personal expansion and fulfillment in conflict with restricting convention, sometimes mistaken for morality.

Adrian Frank, in *The Impressions Of A Cousin* (1883), sacrifices his fortune to win the girl he loves. Eunice's reply to his proposal of marriage is that if he loves her the greatest thing he can do to please her is to marry her cousin Catherine. Adrian is wealthy, and Catherine has just been impoverished by Adrian's half brother, Mr. Caliph, the trustee of Catherine's estate. Eunice has always been poor and can therefore bear to remain poor, but she knows that Catherine, used to riches, will not be able to endure poverty. So she asks Adrian to marry Catherine. Catherine, however, loves Mr. Caliph. Adrian then secretly gives his fortune to his half brother on the condition that he restore Catherine's money to her and then marry her. In this way Adrian removes Eunice's reason for wanting him to marry Catherine. It is Eunice's generosity and unselfishness, in trying to pass on to her friend in need the fortune which Adrian's proposal places at her feet, that inspires Adrian to the romantic and apparently quixotic sacrifice.

Peter Baron, in *Sir Dominick Ferrand* (1893), finds it within his power, by the odd chance of finding a packet of old letters in a secret drawer of an old desk, to blast the reputation of a great public leader who had died some twenty years ago. It will, furthermore, be of great financial benefit to Peter to expose the great historical figure (Sir Dominick Ferrand) to disgrace, as the editor who has rejected Peter's short-story manuscripts will not only purchase the Ferrand letters for a great sum but will also agree to publish Peter's short stories. Peter however questions himself as to whether or not he has the moral right to so interfere in the life of another man, even though that life now merely subsists in the historic minds of a later generation. The woman with whom he is in love (she does not know of his packet of letters or the problem they face him with) mysteriously recedes from his advances when Peter is leaning towards a decision to sell the letters, and she just as mysteriously welcomes his courtship when Peter's momentary inclination is to destroy them. Since he knows that Mrs. Ryves is not cognizant of the letters, Peter naturally does not notice the repeated coincidences. We the readers, however, feel that the occult is at work, or that we are beholding an actual case of parallelism without interaction. As they shuttle back and forth in their respective valleys of decision, Peter and Mrs. Ryves seem to behave as though they are attached to each other by some active but indiscernible mechanism of cause and effect.

Peter finally concludes that Sir Dominick's private life is none of his business, and that he cannot, without dulling his own sensibilities, perform such an aggression on another human being to gain a monetary or other benefit to himself. Shortly after he has burned the letters, Mrs. Ryves informs him that she has decided to accept his proposal of marriage, provided that he still wants to marry her after hearing what she has to tell him. Imagine his astonishment, then, at learning from Mrs. Ryves that the secret of her life is that she is a natural daughter of Sir Dominick Ferrand.

Margaret Hamer, in *The Given Case* (1900), learns that compassion is the clue to conduct by attentively observing the effects of conduct identical to hers in another situation similar to her own. Both Margaret and her friend, Mrs. Kate Despard, are under prior obligation to lovers who have unconscionably neglected them, and both women hesitate to replace the absent lovers with the new ones now present and ardently urging their cases. Margaret's opportunity to study her own conduct objectively and in perspective comes when she is approached by Kate's lover, Barton Reeves, with a request that she intercede for him with her friend Kate. He is entirely unaware, as he eloquently pleads his case in describing Kate's treatment of him, that Margaret herself is treating another man, Philip Mackern, in exactly the same way. As she listens to Barton she thinks of Philip, and learns by an imaginative substitution of Philip for Barton how her own lover must feel.

When Kate, refusing to listen to Margaret's intercession, dismisses Barton, Margaret marries Philip—out of a mysteriously mingled compassion for both men. She had solved her own problem by means of an imaginative and sympathetic projection of herself into the lives and feelings of others.

Maggie Verver, in *The Golden Bowl* (1904), becomes aware of the hard fact that an extremely ugly situation—ugly for any one however inured to the ways of the hard world, but especially and transcendently ugly for one such as Maggie who had lived a sheltered life acquainted only with innocence —had closed in upon her. Her husband, Amerigo, was carrying on an illicit and clandestine love affair with her father's second wife, Charlotte. Moreover, this affair was a resumption of one that had originated long before either she or Charlotte had married their present husbands. A situation of this character is admittedly one of the thorniest and most nerve-trying in the experience of human beings living in close relationship with one another, and it almost always inevitably ends in a crash which makes wreckage of the lives of several people.

Why didn't it happen so in this case?

The answer is simply that all of the people involved in this situation—Maggie Verver and her father Adam, Amerigo,

Charlotte, and Fanny Assingham, the confidante of them all —were deeply guided in all their conduct by a tender care and regard, even in the most trying circumstances, for the feelings of others. This motive in conduct appears and re-appears in microcosmic replica almost everywhere we look throughout the novel, reproducing in miniature the guiding and controlling motive which held Maggie inert and still in her great struggle with herself on first realizing the fact of her husband's and her stepmother's adultery. The very existence of the hideous fact at the heart of the situation, Amerigo's affair with Charlotte, was due to Amerigo's pity for Charlotte as the young and vital wife of a sexless old man. Adam had married Charlotte mainly in order to allay Maggie's fears that her marriage had left him lonely and forsaken. One of Amerigo's and Charlotte's principal cares in their affair was to conduct it with sufficient discretion as to protect Maggie from suffering any hurt feelings. Amerigo discontinued his relation with Charlotte as soon as he discovered that Maggie had divined its existence. Adam Verver probably knew of the affair, but he kept silent about it for fear of bringing it to Maggie's pained attention. By denying the truth of Maggie's assertion that there was something peculiar about the identity of Amerigo's and Charlotte's points of view about everything, Fanny Assingham delayed Maggie's full awareness of the affair, thereby giving her time to prepare an inner resistance to the coming blow, of the imminence of which she was dimly aware. Maggie's motive in not pulling the house down over their heads when she came to full realization of the horrid truth was not only a tender

73

regard for her father's peace of mind, her resolve to so arrange things as never to cause a look of dismay to appear on her father's face, but also a desire to save Fanny Assingham from a lifetime of self-accusation for having first introduced Amerigo to her. Maggie protects her father at Charlotte's expense from the brutal knowledge of the evil in their family life, but she does it in such a way as to help Charlotte not to appear defeated.

In this novel we see self-mastery to be a governing of the emotions by a stronger feeling, poise and true serenity to be passion controlled by considerateness for others, and refined living to be due not to weakness of emotion or mere obedience to external form but to a deep care for others' personal rights. Since regard for the feelings of others is not only a principle of conduct in its major aspects but also in its minor ones— the minutiae of conduct which go by the name of manners— and since regard for the feelings of others is the living heart of decorum as well as of morality, a facile and deceptive logic can appear to confuse these two applications of the principle in a definitive statement of the theme of *The Golden Bowl*. Adequate critical reflection, however, on the sources of conduct within the moral reach of people as real as those in *The Golden Bowl* will enable a responsible reader to comprehend the resplendent lovableness of Maggie and her friends.

In each one of these stories, the inspiration for affirmative action is found in the emotion of compassion, and the gains far outweigh the losses; just as, in James's stories of coercion, the losses far outweigh the gains. This contradicts not, but transcends, the trite deduction of the prosaic realist that the good are defeated while the evil flourish. It depends on what your values are and on whether or not you actually believe in them. For James, these people are real because their values are sound. To argue that these people are romantic because their values are uncommon is to confound the realistic with the average. These stories extol the virtue of compassion as a motive for conduct, demonstrate its practical beneficence as a working force in personal and social relations, and display the intricate and private pathways in the sensibilities of persons thus governed.

The sixteen stories analyzed in this chapter progress from instances of revenge forsworn to rehearsals of repentance for intervention in others' lives and from illustrations of regard for sensibilities different in fibre and quality from one's own to chronicles of compassionate conduct. These four regions of transit in human lives correspond to four stages of reflection or degrees of awareness. This fertilizing interaction between fellowship in feeling and clarity of consciousness is not only the underlying subject common to all of the stories in this group but also the fundamental assertion at the root of all James's fiction.

Chapter Three

LOVE—THE DETERRENT TO THE FULL LIFE

THE JAMESIAN analysis and appraisal of love is one of the great surprises in the history of fiction. That it is a disagreeable surprise, even to some very astute people, the acidulous though scant and gingerly remarks made during the last forty years by readers of *The Sacred Fount*, James's principal love story, bear sufficient witness. Personal-romantic-sexual love, after having been for centuries one of the staple subjects of all forms of literature, had finally, in the nineteenth century, supplanted even religion itself at the crest of man's hierarchy of values. That even a modern master of prose fiction has dared to call into question the real worth of this universally acclaimed goddess is a remarkable phenomenon.

Although it was not until 1901 that James made his complete and definitive statement on the subject of love, his very earliest stories betray a suspicion that the influence of the esteemed goddess on human affairs may not be as beneficent as is generally supposed. These suspicions, however, are not very offensive to his readers because, instead of attacking the goddess herself, they merely reaffirm the received and acknowledged truth that the difficult task of establishing a happy relation with her results so frequently in failure. The door remains open for that forlorn hope voiced in the universal cry: "If certain things could only have been different. . . ." *The Sacred Fount*, however, closed that door—and to this day James's public has never forgiven him.

I

One of James's less direct attacks on the cherished emotion appears in three stories written in 1868, 1878, and 1893. They agree in considering love to be a mysterious malady, as destructive as a disease. The ease with which this concept can be translated by a reader into mere pangs of unassuaged desire saved James from the condemnation which acceptance of his literal meaning would have earned for him. The stories, however, mean what they say.

Margaret Aldis, in *De Grey: A Romance* (1868), having fallen in love with Paul De Grey, is advised by Father Herbert, a close friend of the De Grey family, to renounce Paul and flee, because an ancient curse had caused the death of one member of each pair of lovers involving a De Grey since the time of the Crusades. Margaret decides to brave the curse, refusing to abandon Paul and believing that the curse will be impotent in her case. It is soon apparent, however, that the curse is operating, for Paul goes into a swift decline, and, before they can be married, he dies. Margaret then goes permanently insane.

Diana Belfield, in *Longstaff's Marriage* (1878), refuses, with a cruel jibe, to marry Reginald Longstaff, who has proposed to her on what he thinks is his deathbed. Diana does not know that her cruel manner of rejecting his proposal gives him the strength to conquer his sickness, but when she meets him again two years later she is overjoyed to find that he is alive, because she had fallen in love with him after having spurned his offer of marriage. Longstaff, however, does not renew his offer, having conquered his love along with his sickness, and in consequence Diana in her turn becomes seriously ill. When she is about to die, she sends for Longstaff and asks him to mercifully marry her. Out of pity for her he does so, and even begins to fall in love with her again. But Diana does not recover her health; she grows steadily weaker and soon dies. In the lives of both Diana and Longstaff, love has been no better than a malignant disease.

Louisa Chantry, beautiful and twenty, in *The Visits* (1893), upon meeting at a week-end party a boy of her own age by the name of Jack Brandon, suddenly finds herself writhing so fiercely under the evil spell of sex desire that she approaches Jack in secret and makes importunate amorous advances to him. He gently fends her off and on the following day she reviles him and tells him that he fills her with horror. After Louisa has returned home from her week-end party, she is so overcome with shame at her immodesty in her first interview with Jack Brandon, and at her cruelty to him in her second, that she falls ill. She cannot understand herself; under the compelling power of impulses that she cannot recognize as rightly belonging to her, she had done and said things for which she cannot accept the responsibility. She cannot compel herself to tell either her mother or her doctor what had happened to her, and she finally dies (symbolic death of maidenhood), a resentful victim of a power mysterious, incalculable, irresponsible, capricious, recondite, stronger than herself, and careless of her happiness.

II

These three stories assume love to be a fearful visitation, one of the hazards of human existence, a power to be avoided or placated. In one early novel, James attempts to discover, not very successfully, whether the disastrous visitation might not be circumvented by a widening of the age differential between the lover and the beloved.

Roger Lawrence, in *Watch And Ward* (1871), having utterly and finally failed (at the age of twenty-nine) to win Isabel Morton, an accomplished woman slightly older than himself, to be his wife, adopts into his household Nora Lambert, a girl of twelve and an orphan, with the intention of making her his wife when she reaches a marriageable age. He plans to educate her and mold her character, to be an exemplary companion to her and, finally, her freely chosen husband. When she is eighteen, Nora is taken to Europe by Isabel Morton (now Mrs. Keith and a widow) for a year's tour. A teen-age girl when she leaves, Nora returns a grown and charming woman, ready for marriage. Roger presently speaks to her in the role of suitor, only to see her recoil from him in pained bewilderment. Mrs. Keith, however, comes to Roger's assistance and helps Nora to erase the traces of the daughter-father feeling she has had for Roger. After a time Nora discovers for herself that she does now love Roger in a connubial manner, and she eventually marries him.

III

The economic aspect of love and marriage hovering in the near background of this early novel occupies the foreground in the three short stories that follow and prevents or at least hinders a purely emotional solution to an emotional predicament. The narratives illustrate the usually disheartening and inextricable entanglement of love and marriage with economic considerations, the inseparable mingling of gold and dross.

Locksley, in *A Landscape Painter* (1866), learns after his marriage to Miriam Quarterman that, in spite of all the elaborate precautions he had taken to be known to her only as a poor landscape painter, she had discovered long before his proposal of marriage that he possessed an income of $100,000 per year. Now he will never know to what degree her knowledge of his wealth influenced her decision to accept him as her husband.

Guy Firminger, in *Lord Beauprey* (1892), had long been in love, though dimly aware of it, with Mary Gosselin and she likewise with him but glowingly aware of it; so Mrs. Gosselin, Mary's mother, feels that she is justified when, after Guy has, by means of a series of family deaths, become the very wealthy Lord Beauprey and consequently is much beset by husband-hungry debutantes, she takes the bold step—seeing that one of the predatory matrimonial traps is about to snap on the unwilling Guy—of announcing to the newspapers the engagement of her daughter Mary to marry Lord Beauprey. Guy had actually proposed this device, half in fun, to Mary sometime previously, as a stratagem which would cause the plotting debutantes and their wily mothers to desist. But she, angry at him both for having failed to see that she had wanted to marry him long before he had become wealthy and for failing to see it even now, had at that time refused to be a party to the pretense. Guy is delighted at Mrs. Gosselin's ruse, whereas Mary is displeased but acquiescent. Her relation with Guy has, however, become so complicated by this time, so tarnished by the sordid marriage scramble in which he has so obtusely permitted her to be implicated, that she presently takes the desperate turn of marrying a Mr. Bolton-Brown, an American whom she had but recently met and with whom she had gone over to America to live. This rudely awakens Guy to a belated realization that he has been in love with Mary for many years, but he awakens too late. He and she are victims of the clouding of the marriage issue (rightfully an emotionally determined association only) by economic considerations.

Flora Saunt, in *Glasses* (1896), refuses to wear the unsightly eyeglasses which are her only means of averting the total blindness threatening her. She wants to marry Lord Iffield, a man of great wealth and eminent position, and she knows that he will not propose if he learns of her damaged eyesight. George Dawling loves her utterly and will marry her whether she goes blind or not, but Flora is after bigger game. It is a race for her between blindness and the securing of Lord Iffield fast in marriage. She succeeds in winning a proposal of marriage from Iffield and the engagement is announced in the papers, but before the wedding can take place Iffield learns about the flaw in his beautiful fiancée and

81

repudiates the engagement—"he returned the animal as unsound." Flora fights a losing battle against blindness, finally going stone-blind, whereupon she gladly accepts George Dawling as her husband. In striking Flora Saunt blind, James takes symbolic revenge on the race of women for not valuing above everything else the love that men can give them.

IV

The deadly consequences of a love miscarried, whether from economic or other causes, is the sinister subject of several stories. The danger of committing oneself to a love trial may give one pause when the deeper the commitment the more certainly the price of failure will exceed the worth of any prize won. These stories do more than counsel caution: they subtly mitigate esteem for an aspiration which, defeated, can so turn upon its subject and exact a toll extreme, drastic, and deadly.

Gertrude Whittaker, in *Poor Richard* (1867), and her three suitors all try and all fail to find in love a satisfactory solution to their lives. Richard Clare had asked her many times to marry him, but she could not get romantically excited about this neighbor boy whom she had known from childhood. Gertrude wants to marry Capt. Edmund Severn, but he is too proud to marry a girl so much richer than himself. He goes away to war and is killed. Major James Luttrel, however, is a fortune hunter who wants to marry a rich wife. After Severn is killed, Gertrude sadly accepts Luttrel's proposal of marriage, only to cancel her engagement later upon learning from Richard the true nature of Luttrel's feeling for her. Gertrude would now, should he propose marriage to her again, gladly accept Richard as her husband; but the suffering she had caused him had consumed and burnt away the love he had once felt for her. Richard, too, goes away to war. All four of these people have been hurt by love in one way or another, and the deduction seems inevitable that they would all have been better off without it.

Ferdinand Mason, in *A Most Extraordinary Case* (1868), while slowly but successfully convalescing in the house of his aunt from a serious illness, falls in love with his aunt's adopted niece, Caroline Hofmann. He does not betray his feelings to any one, meaning to recover his physical fitness before he tells Caroline that he loves her, and he therefore remains unaware of the fact that his doctor, Horace Knight, is courting Caroline. When Ferdinand is almost a well man and nearly ready to reveal to Caroline his feeling for her, she announces her engagement to marry Horace Knight. Ferdinand suffers an immediate relapse, his condition grows steadily worse, and in spite of his doctor's efforts and to his doctor's mystification, he finally dies. Cupid had taken advantage of him while he was a convalescent too weak to fight, and the blow killed him.

Maurice Glanvil, in *The Wheel Of Time* (1892), flees from the homely face of Fanny Knocker, the girl who loves him and who nearly dies of disappointment and blighted hope. Twenty years later, Maurice's beloved daughter Vera, whose face is as homely as Fanny's had been, meets and falls in love with Fanny's son Arthur, who bolts in his turn, just as

Vera's father had done before him. Fanny had recovered, to become one of the most charming women, in spite of her homely features, that Maurice had ever known; but Vera dies, the innocent victim through whom Maurice is dealt retributive poetic justice, and love thus once again succeeds in placing a human being at the mercy of an unfortunate triviality.

The narrator of *The Friends Of The Friends* (1896), repudiates her engagement to marry her fiancé because she fancies that the ghost of a dead woman visits him every day. When he dies a few years later she is sure that he had committed suicide in order to keep company as a ghost with the dead woman. The fiancé and the dead woman had had one experience in common: each had seen the ghost of a parent before being notified of the respective deaths. The narrator, acquainted with both people, had often arranged for them to meet so that they could compare experiences, but none of the arranged meetings had taken place. However, the night the woman died her ghost visited the narrator's fiancé. This common power of her friends to see ghosts preys on the narrator's mind to such an extent that they become bracketed in her imagination and predestined lovers by implication.

Mary Tredick, in *The Tone Of Time* (1900), accepts a commission, through an intermediary, to paint an imaginary portrait of a good-looking man under forty years of age, well-dressed in the style of twenty years previous, with the further proviso that the painting is to look as though it had been painted twenty years ago. When the intermediary calls for the completed painting, he finds that it is a masterpiece, representing an insolently handsome man incapable of suffering. He compliments Mary Tredick highly, whereupon she bursts into tears and declares that the portrait was painted in hate. It is apparent that Mary had painted from memory the face of a man whom she had loved, and been wronged by, in her youth. The intermediary then takes the portrait to Mrs. Bridgenorth, who nearly collapses at her first sight of it. It develops that the portrait is the exact image of the very man that she had had in mind when commissioning the work. He was to have been her husband but had died during their engagement, which had been unduly prolonged due to his entanglement with another woman, who must have been Mary Tredick. Mrs. Bridgenorth likes the portrait so well that she doubles the stipulated price, whereupon Mary suspects that Mrs. Bridgenorth is the woman for whom her lover had deserted her, and she refuses to relinquish the portrait to her at any price. The liveliness of Mary Tredick's jealousy after twenty years and the motive alone of Mrs. Bridgenorth's commission reveal the depths of the wounds which love had inflicted on these two women.

V

The frequent conflict between the woman in a man's life and the career of his choice forms the basis of another Jamesian indictment of love. Woman as the object of love rivals creative work in the arts and sciences in the quantity of time and degree of concentrated attentiveness each requires. James's four stories on this subject concur in asserting the incompatibility of these rivals for a man's regard. In each story, a man tries to make room for both, only to find finally that one has shouldered the other out.

Thomas Ludlow, in *A Day Of Days* (1866), on the afternoon previous to the morning on which he is to sail for Europe to begin there his long-planned five-year course of scientific studies, meets—and desperately resists falling in love with—Adela Moore. By their quick attraction for each other, Adela is momentarily endowed for Thomas with, and becomes the purposeful and charming embodiment of, the force and power of romantic-sexual love, exposure to which proves to be a disturbing, mischievous, and powerful temptation to the young scientist. Adela and he spar around with the idea, heroic, poetic, chivalric, of his missing his steamer for her sake; but at the last instant he kisses her hand and goes quickly away, thus wresting his career, as though only by dint of a quick turn of his wrist, from the very jaws of peril.

Benvolio, in the story of that name (1875), produces creative work, of a high poetic order, only during those years in which he woos alternately, but without marrying either one, the two girls who love him. As soon as he chooses one and marries her, his power to write deserts him and his career as a poet comes to an end. The story is also an allegory of the effect on an artist of the social life (represented by the Countess) and the studious life (represented by Scholastica); but the significant element in it as here noted is that it is a love-versus-career pattern in which James casts his allegory.

Dr. Jackson Lemon, in *Lady Barbarina* (1884), marries Lady Barb, daughter of Lord Canterville, and they establish residence in New York City, where Jackson resumes the medical research to which he had before his marriage devoted his abilities and his large inherited fortune so successfully as to have become one of the leading men in his chosen field. Lady Barb, however, cannot become acclimatized to life in America. She can understand neither the challenging competitive rivalry of the New York social queens nor the scientific laboratory interests of her medically minded husband, activities which had both been foreign to her girlhood experience as a daughter of the British aristocracy. When, finally, her little sister Agatha, who has been staying with her on an extended visit, elopes with a bumptious and penniless Texan by the awful name of Herman Longstraw, Lady Barb can bear no more. She bolts, and sails for England. When we last hear of Dr. Jackson Lemon, he is still living in London the idle life of the British aristocracy, his scientific career sacrificed to the sheltered social chrysalis from which he had failed to extricate his wife.

Paul Overt, the young novelist in *The Lesson Of The Master* (1888), falls in love with Marian Fancourt during the same week in which he meets Henry St. George, the great novelist whom he recognizes as his Master. Henry St. George praises Paul's first novel and advises the young writer not to marry Marian but to devote his life to his art. The great writer points to himself as a living proof of the incompatibility of marriage with the artistic career: the need of money with which to support wife, children, and home had compelled him to write potboilers, to suffer a progressive decline in the quality of his art. He persuades Paul to postpone a decision on marriage, at least until after he has written another novel.

Paul accordingly goes to Europe, spends two years there writing a novel, and returns only to find Marian Fancourt and Henry St. George engaged to marry, St. George's first wife having died in the meantime. Had St. George slyly tricked him and stolen his girl from him? Paul struggles with the impact of the blow, but he finally concludes that the Master is right: that it is better to be dedicated to intellectual than to physical passion.

VI

These four animadversions on that popular idol of poet and peasant alike, personal-romantic-sexual love, did not alienate James's public. Love itself can still stand as the greatest value, the most desirable among the experiences possible to man, even though it wrecks careers when it gets the right of way, wrecks lives when it is blocked, spoils quickly by reason of its corrupt association with wealth-sharing, and manifests itself as a sickness in its stricken victims. These four truths about the power of Venus may even add to the awe she inspires in her believers.

That James's intention, however, was to search out the truth about love, not only by annotating some of its external and public imperfections but also by following it into the dark and infected recesses where it lives and has its being, becomes clear when the above stories are considered in the light of *The Awkward Age* and *The Sacred Fount*. In these two stories James tried the hard and thankless task of convincing us that we are not, as we suppose, suffering from temporary dementia but enjoying an interval of sanity when we cry to be relieved from our abject subjection to the emotional turbulence of a romantic love. The unpopularity of these two novels, the unbecoming animosity with which the critical public has viewed them, ironically reflects our desire to see our follies celebrated rather than our illusions exposed. The reality of love, so painstakingly surveyed in *The Sacred Fount*, proves to be so incongruous with our idea of it that we prefer to retain our idea rather than to accept the reality.

A short story written ten years earlier than *The Awkward Age* and thirteen years before *The Sacred Fount* may serve as a prologue to both novels, in that it prefigures the theme to which they give more exhaustive treatment. Oliver Lyon, in *The Liar* (1888), again meets Everina Brant (now Mrs. Capadose) about a dozen years after she had refused to marry him. After making the acquaintance of her husband, Col. Clement Capadose, Oliver soon discovers that the man whom Everina had preferred to him possesses an astonishing defect of character: he is constitutionally unable to tell the literal truth about anything whatsoever. Since he remembers Everina to have been the very soul of veracity, Oliver wonders what effect her husband's disability has had on her. He observes her narrowly when discrepancies between her and her husband's account of any incident are exposed, but he fails to detect any betrayal of embarrassment or sense of humiliation, or even any awareness of her husband's strange foible. Oliver takes pains to become very well acquainted with her again, but never once does she break down and confess to him the humiliation she must feel at being married to a liar. Finally Oliver paints Col. Capadose's portrait, and every line of it exposes the Colonel's penchant for unveracity. When Everina sees the portrait for the first time, she is unaware of Oliver's concealed presence in the room, and she breaks into tears, sobbing, "It's cruel—O it's too cruel!" Oliver is satisfied then that she is aware of her husband's character blemish. The Colonel immediately destroys the painting and when, later on, both Everina and the Colonel lie to him about their opinion of the portrait and their destruction of it, Oliver is convinced that marriage had altered Everina's quality and dulled her sense of truth.

Vanderbank (Van), in *The Awkward Age* (1898), refuses, finally, to marry Nanda Brookenham. Yet he has every inducement to do so: Nanda loves him—she has turned down an offer of marriage from Mitchy, who is a millionaire, because she has chosen Van in her heart—and Mr. Longdon, Nanda's godfather, has told Van that he intends to will his rich fortune to Nanda. Van's only income is his salary. Moreover, Van will probably never love another girl as much as he loves Nanda. But, in spite of all the pressure from within and from without, and in spite of all the inducements, in the end Van withdraws. Nanda will probably never marry, since her love for Van is too deep. Why doesn't Van marry her?

The answer is that it is Van's deepest nature to want to participate in life as a free and untrammeled observer rather than as a contender in the arena. Van had enjoyed his status in Mrs. Brook's drawing-room when he and Mitchy (before Mitchy's marriage to Aggie) and Mrs. Brook and the rest of the "little set" had been able to freely discuss as independent minds any subject under the sun. Conversation and thought had not been hampered by any consciousness of personal emotional involvements on the part of any one of them. Mitchy's freedom of mind, however, vanishes as soon as he marries Aggie. Van keeps himself free from marriage because he fears that marriage, a vested interest, would inevitably modify the range of his thought and the candor of his perception.

The theme of *The Sacred Fount* (1901), is the effect which the emotion of sexual-romantic love has on the two individuals involved in the relation. By "the sacred fount" James means the power which enables a person to retain his bearings in life and to see life with an accurate and disinterested eye. It is James's contention that sexual-romantic love plays havoc with one's desire, one's will, and one's power to see and understand the world. Both the lover and the beloved have given hostages to happiness and are therefore no longer free agents in the search for truth, no longer accurate instruments of perception. If we are loved, the consequent inflated and distended exuberance drains us of the desire for truth, and if we love we are drained of the power to seek truth. James deposes romantic love from its position as the supreme motive for living, as the value which alone endows life with purpose, and opposes to it the life of the mind, the love of truth for its own sake. Since romantic love, when once it gets its grip on a person, will tolerate the operation of no other motive in that person's life, and since it is so all-absorbing and explosive an element in the life of its votary and victim, no creative artist—who by the very nature of his work must see the world truly—can afford to risk subjection to it.

Intellectual adventure versus romantic adventure is the theme of *The Sacred Fount*.

The story form in which, to give the illusion of movement, this thesis is cast consists of a search by the narrator (James himself) for the identity of the mistress of Gilbert Long. The clue to her identity is furnished by the analogy between the effect of Grace Brissenden on her husband, Guy, and that of Gilbert Long on May Server. It is apparent that since he had last seen them something unprecedented had happened to these four people. Grace, really thirteen years Guy's senior, has grown much younger and prettier, while Guy has grown alarmingly old. Gilbert, who used to be so stupid, has become astonishingly brilliant. And May, once one of the most poised and restful of women, is now feverish, nervous, and depleted. In Guy Brissenden and May Server he sees "as he had never seen before what consuming passion can make of the marked mortal on whom, with fixed beak and claws, it has settled as on a prey." And in Grace Brissenden and Gilbert Long he sees the agents of the sacrifice, bloated by their accession of youth, beauty, and brilliance, living parasitically at the expense, emotionally, of their victims.

Grace had agreed with the narrator that May was Gilbert's mistress, but when she begins uncomfortably to sense the analogy between herself and Gilbert in their respective roles, she tries to throw dust in the narrator's eyes by denying that May is the woman. She even goes to the length of deliberately retracting her previous assertion, in agreement with his, that there has been any change in Gilbert Long. But the narrator knows that she is abandoning, in self-protection—as one member of a love couple—her intellectual integrity; he has checked and verified his impressions of the changes in these people by discussing them with Ford Obert, an independent and competent observer.

The narrator protects May's secret, by pretending to agree with Grace and by deliberately misleading Ford Obert, because his motive is not merely to find and identify a hypothetical lover but rather to understand and appreciate what it is like to be in love, to assess with the level regard of an attentive, unsubverted, and sovereign observer the true nature of the effect of sexual-romantic love on the people who experience it.

VII

These three stories, and especially *The Sacred Fount*, embody the most direct and succinct statement of the Jamesian conception of love. Their adverse tenor is somewhat softened in three epilogue-like stories, in which James seems to grant that love may be a resource for the defeated or the retired. These elegiac narratives express the sense of refuge from a hostile world which has been one of the traditional gifts of love to its favored few.

Stuart Straith and Mrs. Harvey, in *Broken Wings* (1900), find themselves, by a fortuitous accident, seated side by side in the theater. They have not met for ten years. In that past time they had been in love; but, by mutual tacit consent, they had dropped each other's acquaintance, each assuming that the other was launched in too successful a career (he as a painter and she as a writer) to entertain the fancy of engaging in any such distracting activity as married life. Tonight at the theater, ten years later, they find, to their mutual surprise, that neither one has had a successful career. His had dwindled from that of painter to that of designer of theatrical costumes, and hers from novelist to reviewer of plays. Their dormant love springs back into life and they decide to pool their resources. They marry, now that each is sure that the other has no strenuous artistic career to labor at.

White-Mason, in *Crapy Cornelia* (1909), upon entering the drawing room of the wealthy young widow, Mrs. Worthingham, to whom he intends today to propose marriage, finds there a friend of his youth, Cornelia Rasch. They renew their acquaintance, and common memories come crowding to their minds. Mrs. Worthingham, in her early thirties, does not and cannot know any of the things that White-Mason and Cornelia Rasch, whose memories reach back nearly fifty years, know about the old New York, when the social center was not in the fifties but between Washington Square and Thirtieth Street. Mrs. Worthingham belongs to the parvenu world that had moved in on the old New York that he and Cornelia knew. The contrast between Cornelia's mind, stocked with the same memories as his, and Mrs. Worthingham's, wanting because of its short reach of experience, makes it clear that the younger woman will always be a stranger to him.

He forgets to propose to Mrs. Worthingham and begins paying daily visits to Cornelia. He and Cornelia see with the same eyes, see the contemporary modern New York in the light of the old, and that is what he would never have been able to do with Mrs. Worthingham. He soon feels certain that deeper satisfaction is in store for him from a close friendship with Crapy Cornelia than from marriage to the wealthy young widow, and so he abandons his wedding plans.

Herbert Dodd, in *The Bench Of Desolation* (1910), retracts his engagement to marry Kate Cookham, because he feels that the intellectual sympathy which had drawn them together had turned on her part, as the date of the intended wedding drew near, into a frightening psychological avidity for him. She thereupon threatens to sue him for breach of promise unless he pays her a certain sum of money. He pays; but, because of this enforced settlement of his emotional account with her, he now hates her. After she has gone to live in a large and distant city, Herbert cultivates mildly the friendship of Nan Drury, a younger and prettier but stupider girl than Kate. Her father's sudden bankruptcy throws Nan on Herbert's hands and he is compelled to marry her, although he is too poor to support a wife. They have two children, and live a shabby poverty-stricken life, Nan often berating him for having permitted Kate to blackmail him into relinquishing to her the money he needs to support his family.

Before ten years have passed, Nan and the two children have died, and Herbert is alone again. Kate presently reappears, transformed into a quietly but expensively dressed, worldly woman. She informs him that her purpose in gouging the breach-of-promise money from him had been to make an investment which would multiply his original capital for him, that she had succeeded in accomplishing that purpose, and that a sum five times the size of the one he had paid her was now on deposit in his name in a local bank. He thus learns that what he had originally diagnosed as psychological avidity had really been a fiercely protective and compassionate tenderness for him; and after he has, with some struggle, reconciled his loyalty to his dead wife with his new and truer conception of Kate, he accepts the money. Kate succeeds at the end of her long and patient trial of self-effacement in gaining Herbert's acquiescence in her desire to befriend and cherish him.

The twenty-two love stories assembled and discussed in this chapter disclose a conception of love radically at variance with that of any other major novelist of the later nineteenth or early twentieth century as well as with the prevailing conception among the novel-reading public. James's view of love was evidently conditioned by his cardinal principle that consciousness is the supreme value. To judge the worth of love primarily and finally with sole reference to its instrumental potency in intensifying the consciousness is to find original and illuminating truths about this mighty subject. That they do not comprise the whole truth James's diminished currency, after the publication of *The Sacred Fount*, sufficiently testifies.

Chapter Four

THE SENSE OF THE PAST

THE ARTISTIC and the reforming casts of mind, differing in that the former searches for things to love and commemorate while the latter looks for things to hate and correct, react in accordance with that difference to James's marked tenderness for past life. The one distinct feature about James's interest in the past which would reconcile these quarreling factions is the precise use to which he wholly devotes that interest.

That use is the enriched, magnified, more deeply lived and understood present moment. James loved all present evidences of human living past or present, physical objects or usages of behavior which bear durable witness to conscious existence. His historical interest was sensuous rather than intellectual. An old house that could be gazed at and touched, an old manuscript that had been physically handled by men of a past generation, an ancient domestic custom living on into the present time interested him more than any history book or any currently written account of past events. The temporal horizon existing in our midst excited his imagination, and his choice of England over America as a place to live was due to the greater depth and resonance of the temporal horizon there. To regard his preference for English residence as a flight from the present into some past culture is as shallow as failure to see that the social reformer evades the present by escaping into the future.

James wrote five stories on the subject of the quickened consciousness derived from a sense of continuity with the past, one on the insidious power of the imagination to distort and misuse the past, and three whose subject is the past exorcized and subordinated to present uses. These nine stories expound not only the health and worth of a sense of the past but also its characteristic disorders and excesses.

Clement Searle, in *A Passionate Pilgrim* (1871), lives the final month of his life with his consciousness intensely and actively engaged in all its powers for the first and last time with the one predominant motif which had throughout his lifetime most animated his imagination. The prompting stimulus that had most charmed him was the present visual aspect of physical objects whose life span reached far back through many human generations; the sight and touch of these evidences of the historic past quickened his sense of the present. Clement had lived in a country where these objects were not plentiful. When his doctor informs him that he has but a month or two yet to live before death will overtake him, Clement travels hastily to England, a country which abounds in visual evidences of past human history. There he spends a delirious month, the last and most vibrant of his life, reveling in the sight of domestic and public architecture and other existing materiél of an ancient civilization. Because of his approaching death he sees these things with a preternatural and heightened awareness, and his consciousness enjoys a final climactic intensity of life, an intensity produced by his responsive surrender to the stimuli which excite his sense of the past.

George Stransom, in *The Altar Of The Dead* (1895), maintains the sensitive life of his personal past by keeping a lit candle for each of his dead friends in an alcoved altar of a church. The number of these candles grows year by year, but there is one candle missing. He has never lit one for Acton Hague, the friend of his youth who had done him a great wrong. When Stransom finally becomes acquainted with a woman whom he has often observed communing at his altar, he learns that she had once been Acton Hague's mistress. She also had been wronged by Acton but nevertheless had mourned his memory at Stransom's altar, all the candles there having been combined in her mind into one great candle for Acton. When Stransom tells her that Acton is the only one of his Dead for whom there is no candle, she ceases to commune at his altar. After a long and bitter struggle with himself, Stransom decides that he must accept his entire past, including Acton, for whom a candle is now finally to be lit, symbolizing the triumphant completion of Stransom's effort to unify his personal past.

Mrs. Gracedew, in *Covering End* (1898), finds an impoverished British nobleman about to abandon his fourteenth-century ancestral castle to a wealthy merchant who holds the mortgages on it and also about to discontinue the ancient family custom of representing his county in Parliament; she succeeds in awakening his dormant sense of the beauty not only of his ancestral home but also of the traditional political role of his family. She falls in love with Clement Yule, purchases the mortgages on his house, and marries him.

This story is a plea for a revitalization of British political and social institutions, a plea against the throwing away of the old bottles and for the refilling of them with new wine. Mrs. Gracedew, an American, calls for a reawakened British awareness of the ancient faiths and the ancient beauties of the British way of life and the application of them to whatever problems present themselves in the contemporary world. Mrs. Gracedew is curiously analogous to James himself, and Clement Yule to England; their marriage is James's symbolic union with the country of his adoption.

Frank Granger, in *Flickerbridge* (1902), is raised to a new and higher plane of awareness as a direct result of his experience in forming an acquaintance with a house and household which had remained untouched by change for a hundred years. He had never before encountered such an oasis of the life of the previous century re-enacted in the immediate present, and the event marks an epoch in his life. Adelaide Wenham, the English spinster, and her eighteenth-century house in Flickerbridge awaken in Granger a sense of the past, show him what it had been like to live in that past time, and enliven his sense of continuity with previous human generations. A wholly new vista of perceptions range into his view and endow him with the power to understand how fundamentally at variance his nature really is from that of the girl (The American Adelaide Wenham) whom he had intended to marry. The blossoming of Frank Granger's sense of the past releases him from an emotional dependence on a girl whose imagination was limited to a mere sense of the picturesque.

Lord Theign, in *The Outcry* (1911), is cuffed and buffeted by historical changes because he can conceive of history only as duration and not as flux. Modern and contemporary virtues do not seem to be virtues to him, because they conflict with the ancient ones in which he had been schooled. The precedence of birth over wealth, of individual rights of privacy over national, public, and social rights, of family unity over chaotic personal independence had given way in his time to new forces which were sweeping away the very axioms of his personal world. Affronted and exasperated by his daughter's curt refusal to marry a man he had chosen for her, by a young art critic's impertinent admonition against his disposal of a valuable painting to a rich American collector, by the rich American collector's insistence that he accept for a valuable painting a sum ten times its official valuation, and finally by the public debate in the daily papers regarding his right to sell his private property, Lord Theign denounces these modern encroachments on his ancient rights. His anachronistic conflict with contemporaneity is tragic in that the values he prizes were once real; it is merely the modern context which has made them inoperative and produced new values. The implication in Lord Theign's story is that an unsound sense of the past can petrify one's sense of values and impair rather than nourish one's awareness of the current world.

Marmaduke, in *Maud-Evelyn* (1900), builds his entire life out of materials furnished by an imaginative piecemeal recreation of a personal past which he had in fact never lived. He accumulates by a continuous creative process a personal history which subsists only in a might-have-been world but which becomes for him, by an act of the creative will, the real life of his mind. Marmaduke's seemingly unbridled sense of the past runs riot, but it possesses nevertheless some internal sanity of logic which makes his life as complete as other and more normal lives.

Mr. and Mrs. Detrick are elderly people whose daughter had died at fourteen years of age. When they meet Marmaduke, they think that he would have been a perfect husband for their dead daughter Maud-Evelyn, who would now be, if she had lived, the same age as Marmaduke. They befriend him and he eventually goes to live in their house. He acts and is treated as though he were the son-in-law of the old couple, and the pretense soon becomes habitual. Then, as the years go by, the three of them by imperceptible degrees remold the past. Actually never having seen Maud-Evelyn, since she had died years before he had met the Detricks, Marmaduke is gradually persuaded by the two old people (whose mnemonic grasp on the factual world is none too good) to talk and act as though, first, he had met Maud-Evelyn just before she died, then as though he had been engaged to marry her, then as though he had married her, and finally as though he had lived with her as her husband for some time before her death. This imagined past becomes so real to Marmaduke that he begins to wear mourning as a widower for his dead wife.

Thus does a sense of the past show its force as a source of life, awry in this instance but nevertheless powerful enough to give direction to the whole life of one man.

Marco Valerio, in *The Last Of The Valerii* (1874), falls in love with a marble statue of the Roman goddess Juno which his wife Martha, an American girl, had disinterred from its immemorial grave in the grounds of their Italian villa. Marco falls strangely under the sway of the marble goddess, locks her in a summerhouse, and worships her in secret, forsaking his wife. The sight of Juno has caused him to revert to the ways of his remote Roman ancestors: his galvanized sense of his racial past has lured him away from his immediately present, flesh-and-blood wife.

Martha finally exorcizes the hold of the past on Marco by reburying the Juno in the ground from which she had been excavated; but we who read the story are left with a vivid sense of the stimulation afforded to the historic consciousness by the fragmentary physical remains of ancient Roman art.

Amy and Susan Frush, in *The Third Person* (1900), inherit an old ancestral house which charms them with its evidences of long family history and ancient associations. Not long after the two sisters have begun living in the old house, they discover a packet of musty letters from which they learn that an ancestor by the name of Cuthbert Frush had been hanged for smuggling. This discovery so enlivens their sense of their family's remote past that it materializes in the appearance of Cuthbert's ghost. He lives in the house with them, frequently joining them at their household work. At first they are delighted and honored. But gradually they come to feel ill at ease in their contemporary world, because they fancy that their neighbors are beginning to suspect them of a guilty secret commerce with the past. They try various ways

to exorcize the ghost and finally succeed by smuggling a for-
bidden article through the French customs—in emulation of
the bold deeds, of the old wild kind, done by Cuthbert.

Performance of the same high order as that of their ancestor enabled them to overcome their intimidated awe of
him and to quiet their too vibrant sense of the past.

Ralph Pendrel, in *The Sense Of The Past* (1917), explores
more thoroughly than any other James character that be-
guiling but unsound escape mechanism: the romanticization
of the past. Ralph is possessed of the purest strain of the
sensuous historic consciousness. His imaginative power to
re-create for himself the psychical environment of bygone
times is so strong that not only do ghosts of past presences
materialize for him, but he is also empowered to go back into
an earlier century and physically live there.

He does just that—and his experience there constitutes a
dissolvent analysis of, and an exposure of the weakness of,
the malaise for which a romanticization of the past is the
anodyne. Ralph eventually returns to the present and to his
twentieth-century girl, Aurora Coyne, content at last to live
in his contemporary world. His opportunity to live in the
past century comes when an ancestor—a namesake to whom
he bears a striking resemblance and who was, at the time his
portrait was painted, the same age as Ralph—speaks to him
out of his portrait on the wall and suggests that they exchange lives. The earlier Ralph is just on the point of arriving
home from a long visit abroad and the later one can therefore
step into his life without any obvious hitches. Ralph accepts
the proposal and arrives at the house of his cousins the

Midmores, in the time of Horace Walpole (Sir Cantopher Bland, in the novel). The ways of the eighteenth century are so familiar to Ralph that he intuitively does the right thing at all times. The substitution is not detected, not even by the girl, Molly Midmore, fiancée to the original Ralph.

The trouble begins, however, when he meets Molly's sister, Nan. He finds himself falling in love with the wrong girl. And the reason is that Nan's personal qualities are those of a girl far in advance of her time. Her rarity in the eighteenth-century world is owing to her difference from girls contemporary with herself and her likeness to girls contemporary with Ralph. Nan revives his interest in the modern world, in the twentieth-century timbre of mind. Each feels a mysterious affinity with the other, with the consequence that both of them become aware of the discrepancy between that affinity and Ralph's destined marriage to Molly. Nan divines the truth—that this Ralph Pendrel is not their Ralph at all, but a ghost from the future. Ralph cannot marry her: he has to live the earlier Ralph's life, not some new variation of his own, or else return to his proper time. This he does, because his love of the present, which he had thought dead, has been resuscitated by the modernity of the eighteenth-century girl.

These nine stories make clear the real nature of James's interest in Europe and England. That the removal of his place of residence from America to England was neither a retreat into the past nor a flight from present New World challenges to past Old World solutions but rather an expression of an eagerness to come to closer grips with a present reality more deeply telescoped with time—of this, these stories are the proof. He went to Europe to find deeper soil to thrust his roots into, and these nine stories were the fruit thereof, by which he must be judged.

The peculiar feature common to all of James's stories on the subject of the historic sense is that they are, one and all, even *The Sense Of The Past*, stories of contemporary people living in the contemporary world. None of them can be likened in any way to the conventional historical novel. Consciousness of the living past, embodied in man's behavior and his appurtenances, appears in James's fiction as a factor impregnating and seasoning the consciousness of the present. One wonders if those who so arrogantly press forward into the forefront of time, eschewing everything not of today or tomorrow, enjoy so deep a sense of life as those who, like James, cultivate a sympathetic awareness of that life which, though lived long ago, persists in the tangible present.

Chapter Five

THE ARTISTIC HOMAGE VERSUS
THE LURE OF POWER

THOSE PEOPLE for whom economic wealth, or political
power, or social position are final values to which all
other values must be contributory constitute a type character
as ancient as the human race. The mass of mankind either
gives lip service to or consoles itself with other values which
it in truth and usually in secret deems inferior to at least
one of the above three ends.

A remnant of humanity, curiously oblivious to the desirability of these three great values, has, however, probably
always been present somewhere in human society. This
remnant is composed of saints, scholars, scientists, and artists.
These four classes of people possess a common difference
from the rest of the human race in that they have found a
value which supersedes all three of the values almost universally held to be paramount.

The obscurely motivated behavior of the remnant has been
and is to this day observed by the general with mingled
emotions, which range the gamut from amusement to anger
and from awe to hatred. The privileged few of the official
world, and the many who would be privileged and official if
they could, agree either in contemning or in regarding with
blank bewilderment all who do not act as though wealth,

power, and position are ends in themselves and the only real ends conceivable to sanity.

James did not minimize the incomprehension of the many for the virtues of the few; he knew how stoutly lodged in the public mind was the belief in the substantial worth of these material goods. However, he also knew that the values of the saving few were superior to the values of the many, and he believed that they were valid, not only for saints, scholars, scientists, and artists, but for all people. They were valid, specifically, for his most conscious man, who need not be either saint, scholar, scientist, or artist, but simply a man of generally responsive and civilized intelligence. An expanding consciousness is without exception the real supreme value for all human beings, whether they know it or not, and to this value wealth, power, and position have little or no relevance. Four of James's stories embody this thought, with increasing clarity from story to story.

Mark Ambient, in *The Author Of Beltraffio* (1884), encounters in his wife the deep hostility which the worldly vested interests always feel for the close and inquiring scrutiny of basic values exercised by the race of artists. Beatrice Ambient knows that her husband is regarded as the foremost literary master of his time, but she can not abide his books. To sift life through his mind the way her husband does in his novels seems to Mark's wife a gratuitously corrosive act. She has a child, Dolcino, whose world is being pulled down around his ears by writers such as his father. When Beatrice reads Mark's last masterpiece, her hatred and fear finally become so great that, in order to protect her son from growing up to read his father's contaminating and insidious fiction, she lets the child die during an illness by wilfully neglecting to feed him his medicine.

Dora Temperley, in *Mrs. Temperley* (1889), mutely but successfully opposes her extremely able and ambitious mother, and in her opposition the two take shape as symbols of two fundamentally disparate moral perspectives: the aesthetic and the official. The scale of values implicit in the artistic homage is incongruous with the official esteem for temporal power and position, as the former requires the exercise of consciousness for its own sake while the latter seeks the gratification of self-aggrandizement.

It became Mrs. Temperley's ambition after her husband had died, leaving her a comfortable fortune and three small daughters, to quit the frontier community in which she had lived, educate her daughters, and prepare them for marriage to young men from aristocratic and wealthy families. Her social and economic objectives were so lofty as to be within her reach only if she were an extremely astute, crafty, and diplomatic personage. Mrs. Temperley possessed these qualities, however, and so she eventually gained entree to the society she desired. It was now possible for her to arrange for her three daughters marital alliances with eminent and distinguished families.

An obstacle now plants itself squarely in her path, and she finds herself powerless to dislodge it. Dora, the eldest daughter, refuses to marry for social position; this is particularly dismaying because it is the custom of the society in question to marry into a family of girls only after the eldest has chosen a husband. Dora had been a queer, bookish girl and had been in love from girlhood with an art student named Raymond Bestwick. Mrs. Temperley had kept them separated and had counted on Dora losing interest in the penniless artist upon reaching mature years. It becomes apparent, however, that it is not exactly her love for Raymond that motivates Dora's opposition to her mother's plans. The root of the matter is that Dora does not respect the things in life that her mother respects; she does not place such a high premium on worldly position. She in fact despises her mother's snobbery. She consents not to marry Raymond so long as her sisters remain unmarried, as this mésalliance would further damage her sisters' prospects, but she definitely refuses to marry any one else. The story ends on a note of doubt as to whether any of the three girls will ever get a husband.

The significant point here is that it is acquaintance with the mysterious charm of Art itself which has taught Dora that there are stronger and greater values in life than the puissant panoply of social eminence.

Nicholas Dormer, in *The Tragic Muse* (1889), successfully withstanding temptations and bribes which would have overwhelmed a lesser man, persists at all costs in his activity as a portrait painter. The choice he has to make between a political and an artistic career is especially difficult for him because the rewards of the former are so great and so certain while those of the latter are so problematical and subjective. Since he is the son of a deceased and revered political leader, a political career would be the one most natural for him. His mother's heart is set, not only on his following in his father's footsteps and achieving the position, that of Prime Minister of England, which the elder Dormer had almost reached when he died, but also on his restoring the family income to its once high level. If Nick chooses to remain in politics, Charles Carteret, his godfather, will settle a $300,000 fortune on him, and Julia Dallow, his very wealthy cousin, will marry him. Furthermore, Nick is already a member of Parliament, and he knows that he possesses the ability to accomplish the great things which are expected of him by his political associates as well as by his family and friends.

On the other hand, the one activity which most challenges his powers is that of portrait painting. This he finds much more difficult than anything else that he has tried, and he is by no means certain of his talent as a painter. He merely knows that he enjoys the arduous toil of trying to paint more than he does the prospect of becoming Prime Minister, the possessor of Charles Carteret's $300,000, and the husband of Julia Dallow. He has learned from observing his friend Miriam Rooth, an actress, just how excruciatingly arduous a toil is required of any one who practices a serious art, but this only acts as a spur to his desire to paint.

When Nick finally resigns his seat in Parliament, he is in effect saying that he believes political honor, wealth, and the love of a beautiful woman to be rewards inferior to the charm at the core of any creative art activity, and artistic endeavor to be fundamentally more satisfying than any other because, dealing as it does with really larger issues, deeper truths, and finer experiences, it draws a deeper draft on the whole power of a man.

111

Graham Fielder, in *The Ivory Tower* (1917), consciously and with scrupulous abstention from protest, permits himself to be despoiled of a huge fortune, thereby giving tacit but very real expression to his contempt for those people for whom the accumulation of material gain is the paramount value in life.

The fortune had been willed to Graham by an uncle whom he had never met. He thereafter becomes acquainted with a group of people who had been friends of his uncle, and among them is Horton Vint, a man who had been a college chum of Graham several years ago. The two men renew their friendship, and when Graham, realizing that he himself does not know how to invest his inherited capital, learns that Horton is a business man, he asks his old friend to administer the fortune for him. Horton accepts the responsibility. Graham then mingles freely with the society to which Horton introduces him, and he becomes more and more astonished, disgusted, and horrified at the avid desires of these people to acquire money and at their groveling before him because of his money. The consequence of his growing critical disdain of these money lovers is that, when he learns that Horton is embezzling large sums from him under the pretense of loss by bad investments, Graham feigns belief in Horton's lame explanations for the alarming shrinkage of his capital.

Graham is not an artist, but he possesses the generally responsive and civilized intelligence from which springs the sense of values implicit in the artistic—as opposed to the commercial—homage.

———

Perhaps the most interesting and significant fact about all four of these stories is the powerlessness of the few to render an explanation of itself and to make its grounds of action intelligible to the many. The helplessness of Mark Ambient to penetrate the opacity of Beatrice's mind, the mute obduracy which Dora offered her mother in lieu of self-protective exoneration, the silent sorrow which was the limit of Nick Dormer's communicability with his stricken mother and with Charles Carteret, the stoic resignation with which Graham Fielder permitted the world to continue to consider him a feeble dupe: the moral identity of these four confrontations throws considerable light on James's tough-minded appraisal of the moral status of civilized man. The ingrained wrongheadedness inculcated by our psychosocial environment closes the mind of man, except in rare and exceptional instances, and deprives it of the organ of understanding by means of which superior and true values are apprehended.

Another noteworthy fact about these stories is that James did not sentimentalize his heroes and heroines by showing them as defeated by the powerful and conventional world. Dora, Nick, Graham, and even Mark Ambient triumph over and prove stronger than their opponents. They are strong enough even to be tender with them. Dora tries to let her mother have what she wants—she reserves only the final core of her selfhood; Nick's decision to follow his own course rather than the one mapped out for him by his mother and Julia Dallow and Charles Carteret was reached only after long and grievous deliberation; Graham pities rather than despises his friend and despoiler, Horton Vint; and Mark

Ambient, withholding the sharp and silencing retorts which many of us would forgive him, patiently listens to his wife's exposition of her tawdry conception of art's function in life. But not one of the four finally swerves from the course which his superior, though incommunicable, sense of values holds him to. Each one proves, by decisive trial, to be tougher than those who deem themselves the harder-headed.

The four stories might be considered as James's defense of his profession, of its characteristic outlook on life, and his affirmation that its values must come to supplant the ones now dominant. The aesthetic values are valid not only for the specifically artistic but for all other activities as well. Graham Fielder, the leading figure of his unfinished novel, *The Ivory Tower*, was deliberately dissociated by James from any artistic pursuit in order to emphasize the general validity of the values implicit in the artistic homage. This ambitious, all-embracing, and unrestricted conception in James of the universal relevance inherent in the methodology of the aesthetic function marks him as one artist who is a great humanist also.

Chapter Six

ATTACKS ON THE SHELTERED LIFE

A TOUCHSTONE which will distinguish a son of Uncle Sam from the men of any other nation is the concept of the sheltered life. Mention this concept in a group composed of men from many nations and the first one to show signs of disdain will be the American citizen. Antagonism for the sheltered life and the theory of human excellence for which it stands has been a peculiarly American trait ever since the democratic frontier first sprang into life on this continent. Newcomers to our land acquire this trait as soon as they disembark on our shores, and when Americans visit Europe this trait is the badge of their birthland.

Neither a true upper class nor a true peasantry has come into being in the New World and by the same token the shackles of the sheltered life have never been refitted to the human frame west of the Atlantic shore—except momentarily in our Southern states. The division of human beings into classes by birth fathers the notion that the life of man and woman should be circumscribed from childhood by the boundaries first of family and then of class. Axioms of conduct, emphasizing the refining virtue of carefully restricted experience and the debasing effect of careless exposure to forms of life outside one's tradition, become implanted in the minds of people who live in a society marked by class barriers. The concept and practice of the sheltered life flourishes, therefore, wherever there are aristocrats and peasants, while it tends to vanish wherever class differences cease to exist. In America, impatience with the idea of the sheltered life burgeoned, soon after our declaration of independence, into a national trait.

Conspicuous in his fiction is James's approval of and partiality for that trait. Despite its long exposure to English life, James's American heritage lived lustily on in his many attacks on the principle of the sheltered life. His English residence gave him a chance to observe at first hand the operation of that principle and to contrast with it the large appetite for experience characteristic of his countrymen. His fiction on this subject testifies loudly to the American character of his outlook on life and distinctly marks him as one of the major exemplars and interpreters of the American temper. He denied, as does the whole American nation, that restriction of experience refines and that expansion of experience debases; he denied the virtue of a sheltered life even in its home field—a class society; he affirmed without reserve the opposite principle—that restricted experience debases and expanded experience refines. This theme pervades the following stories.

The narrator of *The Diary Of A Man Of Fifty* (1879), is tormented by evidence which seems to indicate that he had fatally wronged both himself and the girl he loved, Bianca Salvi, when he had twenty-seven years ago, in a jealous rage, abandoned her and gone to India. During those ensuing twenty-seven years he had lived a plain, dull life, thinking that by leaving Bianca he had avoided a great unhappiness.

and now he learns from Bianca's daughter, her namesake and image, that the girl he had forsaken had loved him until the day she died. If this be true, he had rejected a great happiness and forced a wrong life upon both himself and her. True, she had eventually married Camerino, the man of whom he had been so jealous, but Bianca the younger maintains that her mother had done so only because of her true lover's desertion.

The narrator has been urging his young friend, Edmund Stanmer, to desist courting the younger Bianca, because she is probably the image of her mother in character as well as in person and is therefore a mere scientific flirt. But when, three years later, he meets Edmund again, the young man who has been married to Bianca for some time tells the man of fifty, "Depend on it—you were wrong." He is then destined to be forever haunted by the ghost of a past that might have been, the wraith of rejected experience.

The tragic suicide of Hyacinth Robinson, in *The Princess Casamassima* (1885), was due to Hyacinth's unjustifiable meddling in his own life. On the day that Hyacinth irrevocably committed his future on the ground of that day's opinions, he signed his own death warrant. It was as though, thinking he had reached his full growth, he had fastened around himself an iron band which, remaining rigid while he kept right on growing—as human beings have a way of doing—choked him to death. The evil which Hyacinth committed, in taking the vow to assassinate anyone when instructed by his revolutionary leaders to do so at any time during the next five years, was simply that of acting as

though growth and change did not exist, as though matura-
tion were not a process that continued as long as a man lives.
James means by the history of Hyacinth Robinson that a man
has no more right to restrict his own growth than he has to restrict anyone else's, that the right and privilege to grow and
change is the supreme right of all men, that to reserve oneself
and others for possible elevation to higher levels of awareness
is to abide by one of the obligatory laws of human nature.

Maisie Farange, in *What Maisie Knew* (1897), achieves the
power at the very early age of about twelve to make mature
decisions. She derives this power from an acquaintance with
the ways of the world usually denied to youth until after it
has reached manhood and womanhood. Maisie's father and
mother were divorced when Maisie was but six years old,
and the court awarded the child to each parent for alternate
six-month periods until she became of age. Maisie becomes
aware of her parents' extramarital relationships both before
and after their divorce, and of the affair that subsequently
develops between her mother's second husband and her
father's second wife. The tension of the story then consists
in the problematical effect of the knowledge, at such an early
age, of such unorthodox and improper behavior on the
character of Maisie. According to the shelter principle of
child rearing, lack of protection from such knowledge results
in contamination and dulling of the moral sense.

Exposure to this environment, however, develops rather
than corrodes the character of Maisie. Something flowers in
Maisie which is deeper and better than a moral sense—the
power to distinguish the incomplete from the complete

human being. When she chooses to live with Mrs. Wix, her moral old governess, rather than with her cohabiting step-mother and stepfather, her grounds of decision are not the "immorality" of Sir Claude and Mrs. Beale but rather the perception that Mrs. Wix is complete within herself, while Sir Claude and Mrs. Beale are, insofar as they need each other, incomplete. The value to life of the greatest expansion of consciousness possible, even at the earliest of tender ages and no matter what evils are encountered, is the theme of *What Maisie Knew*.

The telegraphist, in *In The Cage* (1898), rescues two of her customers, Capt. Everard and Lady Bradeen, from threat-ened embroilment in public scandal by being able to instantly produce from memory the exact wording of a telegram which had passed between them several months previously. Her power to do them this service and avert exposure of their clandestine love affair was due to her actively sympathetic and imaginative participation in the lives of the people whose telegrams passed through her hands. She did not do a mere routine and mechanical job in her cage: she made use of her strategic position to observe her customers and follow the sense of their telegrams to one another. The messages she transmitted became in her observant mind successive in-stallments in the story of the lives of characters who person-ally presented themselves at her window. She is a particularly sentient being and thereby demonstrates even in her humble station that a high pitch of awareness of, and a sensitive response to, the life within one's reach can create for one a rich and rewarding experience of living.

Maud Blessingbourne, in *The Story In It* (1903), proves to our satisfaction—if not to that of Mrs. Dyott and Col. Voyt, her friends who had challenged her—that she lives an exciting life, and that, although she has no husband or lover nor pursues any observable activity, she nevertheless possesses a consciousness charged with emotions, events, and a lively continuing history. When Col. Voyt and Mrs. Dyott maintain in conversational rivalry with Maud that to be "good" means to go without romance, Maud refuses to concur. We presently learn that her reason for disagreeing with them is that she has been for many years secretly in love with a man who has never become aware of her love for him. She sees him frequently at the houses of mutual friends where she observes him at her leisure, delighting in every move he makes and in every word he utters. Her stored up impressions of him are the contents of her consciousness, and all the days of her life are as beautiful songs to her because of the thought and image and frequently renewed sight of the man she loves. Even though it exists only in her own heart, her romance is real because it gives life to her mind.

John Marcher, in *The Beast In The Jungle* (1903), rejects his last opportunity in life to possess the woman he loves and is loved by, and this ultimate refusal to discard his male virginity destroys his only remaining defense against the final pounce of his fate. The beast leaps when John Marcher, for the last time, fails to take May Bartram in his arms. The unknown fate which during his entire life he had felt was awaiting him and which he had mystically personified as "the beast in the jungle" was simply to be the one man in the world to whom nothing on earth was to happen. He could have evaded this fate by recognizing May Bartram's proffered surrender as the rescue and salvation that it was, but he failed then—as he had failed all his life—to realize that an irremediable offense against life is the rejection of experience: that rejection which is not merely incidental to the process of selection and discrimination but is essentially a refusal to live. John Marcher had curtailed and repressed his life, and he found out too late that in doing so he had lost not only his own appropriate heritage but May Bartram's as well.

Lambert Strether, in *The Ambassadors* (1903), encounters and succeeds in understanding, and thereby mastering, an experience unprecedented in his personal history, and he is consequently lifted to a new level of consciousness from which vistas of living, hitherto closed to him, open to his view. Residing in Woollett, Massachusetts, he had reached the age of fifty without having found it necessary to distinguish an impropriety from an immorality; now, however, he is suddenly called upon to face—and to take a position with respect to it—a hard fact which tests and refines the quality of his mind. He learns that two people whom he knows well and admires extremely for their superlative personal excellences, Chad Newsome and Marie de Vionnet, possess an adulterous relation to each other. The tension in the mind of the reader and in the minds of the other characters in the novel arises from their effort to answer the question: what effect will the impending discovery of this relation have upon Strether? Will he be able to retain his presence of mind, rise to the mental challenge of the occasion,

121

and judge the individual case on its own merits? Or will he judge by rote, recoiling in condemnation and horror from this infraction of the provincial "moral" code to which he is accustomed? Will his mind be able to cut through the barriers of usage, custom, and propriety to a sound and realistic morality? Or will it quail before the papier-mâché prohibitions of a mere conventional morality?

Strether has a few hard moments, but in the end he wholeheartedly endorses the relation and adjures Chad never to forsake his mistress. He sees that Marie's effect on Chad has been eminently good, that he is in fact, as he now stands, her creation, and that she therefore has a vested right to him.

Strether thereby loses his prospective wealthy wife, Mrs. Newsome (Chad's mother), by whom he had been commissioned to fetch Chad home from his Parisian paramour, but Strether's gain is greater than his loss. He sees Mrs. Newsome now for the shallow and inadequately civilized moralist she is, and his newly won, conscious mental grasp on essential values is more precious to him than anything Mrs. Newsome could have given him.

––––––

The burden of thought shared by all seven of these stories, the central idea which vitalizes the entire group, emphatically expresses the desirability of continual addition to the sum total of conscious events which comprise an individual life and the detriment incurred by the erection of boundaries which restrict the quantity of available experience. Both the man of fifty and Jonn Marcher were injured irremediably by resistance to and flight from the life which solicited their participation. Hyacinth Robinson destroyed himself by attempting to halt his experience of life and anchor it to future execution of today's vow. The telegraphist and Maud Blessingbourne managed to fertilize their entire lives by making an unusually complete and thorough use of the limited opportunities for experience available to them. Maisie Farange decisively refutes the superstition that maidenhood excellence depends on the extent of guarded protection from knowledge of the facts of life. And Lambert Strether came to full stature, after nearly a lifetime of arrested development, only after the dearth of experience which had stunted him had been superseded by an abundance of food for his understanding. The sheltered life had almost made a dunce of Strether, but he matured quickly when the shelters were removed.

James's antagonism to the sheltered life, though rooted in his American heritage, issues directly from his conception of the expanding consciousness. It was in the interest of, and as food for, the expanding consciousness that he advocated multiplicity of relations to life. An augmented experience increases the contents of consciousness. This, as we have seen, James identified as the intrinsic aim itself of human existence.

Chapter Seven

THE MYSTERY OF PERSONAL IDENTITY

THE STRICTLY psychological stories of James attempt to define a human being, to describe what in essence a human being really is, in terms of his ability or inability to change, either in his own eyes or in the eyes of the people who observe him. James appears to have been as impressed by the inconstancy of human character as by its persisting sameness. The kaleidoscopic nature of a person or of his context or of both attracted James's curiosity and stimulated him to commemorate that elusive aspect of the psychological scene in a series of remarkable and fascinating studies. The unspoken question which these stories conjure forth and seem to have been written to answer is: Where, if anywhere, in all this flux does personal identity continuingly inhere?

The earliest story on this subject tells of a man who lost his identity when his context changed. Brooksmith, in the story of that name (1891), disintegrates because he has lost his function in life. He had learned to do one thing perfectly, and after that one thing was no longer needed, Brooksmith went rapidly to ruin. He had become a fine and delicate instrument, the use for which had vanished. The blunter uses subsequently available to him could not content him, so he lost his will to live.

Brooksmith's position was that of butler to the aged invalid and retired diplomat, Oliver Offord. But with the passage of time he had become more of a prime minister to his master than a mere servant. Brooksmith stood guard over Oliver Offord, and everyone who came to visit Mr. Offord necessarily saw Brooksmith first. And Brooksmith was more or less present at every gathering of the faithful in the Offord drawing room. He not only officiated in placing the house at the disposal of the guests but he also listened, while he worked, to most of the conversations. The social machinery of the house was noiselessly, effortlessly, unobtrusively, and with supreme tact, operated and supervised by Brooksmith.

Then Mr. Offord died.

We subsequently catch occasional glimpses of the decline of Brooksmith. Bereft not only of his beloved Offord but also of the distinguished bachelor society that had moved through the Offord house, he could not be contented in any of the houses in which he afterwards worked. He helplessly drifts lower and lower in the servant scale, until he becomes merely an extra waiter at public banquets. He finally disappears entirely, we are given to suspect into the Thames. Brooksmith had found himself unable to form any new attachment, to find any setting in which his faculties could function as completely as they had at Offord's house. He had seen and possessed the perfect beauty, and now there was nothing left him but to waste away. Hyacinth (in *The Princess Casamassima*) had two loyalties, which he could not reconcile; Brooksmith was unable to replace the only one he had ever possessed.

Allan Wayworth, in *Nona Vincent* (1892), is rescued from emotional disaster through the agency of the psychological phenomenon known as shifted personal identity. An actress, Violet Grey, so successfully incarnates on the stage the playwright Allan Wayworth's heroine, Nona Vincent, that she sheds her Violet Gray identity and continues to live that of her created character. This phenomenon enables Allan to transfer his emotional fixation from a woman who cannot marry him to one who can. Nona Vincent is Allan's idea of what Mrs. Alsager (with whom Allan has long been in love) would have been like had she not married Mr. Alsager. Violet Grey, at first a failure in playing the part, learns from observing Mrs. Alsager how to act it to Allan's complete satisfaction. In doing so she becomes the person Allan had wanted Mrs. Alsager to be, and thereby, ultimately, his wife. Mrs. Alsager, in love with Allan but unable to marry him herself, helps to create a substitute who can.

Clare Vawdrey and Lord Mellifont, in *The Private Life* (1892), are variant manifestations of the psychological mystery of personal identity. It is discovered that Clare Vawdrey, the brilliant novelist who often appears in public and who does not seem to be in person the man of genius that his books would lead one to expect him to be, possesses a double who never appears in public and who writes the books; it is also discovered that Lord Mellifont, the brilliant statesman who fulfills to perfection the public's estimation of what a brilliant statesman should be, possesses no private identity whatever, no palpable physical existence when there is no public present. Clare Vawdrey's essential personal identity is all private and Lord Mellifont's is all public. When Clare Vawdrey is in his room there are two people there, the solitary writer and the social being; when Lord Mellifont is in his room, there is nobody there—the room is empty.

What this fanciful story emphasizes is that in order to know the essential person one must find him engaged in the one activity which engrosses the whole man or all the powers of the man, that one can know another person fully only by seeing him do what he can do best. The mystery of what a man really is can only be resolved by observation of that activity of his which completely expresses his essential being.

George Dane, in *The Great Good Place* (1900), loses his identity in a dream, and his story has the effect of a certain kind of dream on the reader. Perhaps everyone has awakened some time or other from a dream which seemed immediately afterwards to affect the erstwhile dreamer's surroundings, the people and places of the real world, in an uncanny, weird, eerie sort of way, to make everyone seem a little someone else, and every familiar place somehow changed. The familiar people and places of one's own daylight experience, having been transmuted in the dream into something rich and strange, re-enter one's consciousness upon awakening with lingering, reminiscent traces of the recent enchanted history in which they had figured. These dreams intimate the existence of another world in which everything is the same as in the real one, but somehow ennobled, with all disagreeable elements omitted. They are perhaps the means by which the subconscious heals the too conscious mind.

George Dane was a successful writer, so successful that his correspondence, his luncheon engagements, the miscellany of living detail attendant on success bid fair to absorb his whole life. He was on the verge of a nervous breakdown. Then one morning a young writer to whom success had not yet happened came for breakfast. The next thing Dane knows, he is in a Great Good Place. The young writer had offered to be his substitute and do all his work, to undertake the miscellaneous detail of Dane's life, and he had found this Great Good Place for Dane to rest in. It is not a cloister, or a resort, but something so much better, a great quiet hotel-like institution so managed as to eliminate every conceivable annoyance from a human environment, a sort of Shangri-la. He seems to live there for weeks and then decides that he is ready to leave. At that instant he awakes and finds himself in the same room where he had met the young writer. The young man is sitting at Dane's desk, doing Dane's work, and it is the afternoon of the day on which he had breakfasted with the young stranger. He had merely slept all day, under the soothing influence of his visitor. He now recognizes his servant Brown and the young writer as people who had appeared in the dream disguised as his Brothers in the Great Good Place. His room here in the real world, too, he now sees to be the same room as the one he had had in the Great Good Place; and so the people and places of the real world take on some of the reflected and reminiscential glory of the Great Good Place—which was only a dream. *The Great Good Place* tells of a day's dream of a nervous breakdown, a dream that cleansed and purged as effectively as the original which it simulated.

Abel F. Taker, in *Fordham Castle* (1904), repeats on a reflective level the shedding of identity accomplished by his

wife and another woman on a cheaply ambitious and fraudulent level. His wife had renamed him C. P. Addard, settled
him in a Swiss resort, renamed herself Mrs. Sherrington
Reeves, and then had gone to London. He meets an old
woman whose situation duplicates his: her daughter Maggie
Magaw has renamed herself Lady Dunderton and changed
her mother's name from Magaw to Vanderplank. Abel re-
luctantly gropes his way among these shifting identities, re-
gretful at first for the Abel F. Taker whom he had been
accustomed to be, and then dreading to become the Mr.
Sherrington Reeves that his wife will soon summon forth
from his dead selves. He wants now to remain C. P. Addard.
This story is a poetic, mystical discourse on the joys and
sorrows of change, growth, renewal, the shedding of past
selves, the exfoliation of laminae, the incredible mystery of
the multiple successive personalities we all are.

Julia Bride, in the story of that name (1908), tries desperately to recast her public character, to reconstruct the facts
of her past life so as to render them susceptible of a changed
interpretation, but she finds herself inextricably caught and
fixed in the public mind as the girl who had been engaged to
six successive men and whose mother had had three successive husbands. Julia has fallen in love with Basil French and
she knows that his family will identify her, to her discredit,
as the girl reputed to be so careless of her betrothal pledges.
She nervously tries and abandons a number of expedients,
the hopelessness of her position becoming more and more
apparent to her, until she finally arrives at a state of utter
discouragement. Julia has woven for herself a context from

which she cannot escape, and she learns to her cost that her personal identity is inseparable from the reflection she casts in the eyes and minds of the observant public.

———

The answer which these six stories seem to furnish to the question they seem to ask is that personal identity subsists and has its real life only in the consciousness of observers, only one of which, of course, can be oneself. We are the contents of one another's consciousness as well as mutually dependent sources of the essence of life. The definition of a man is the accumulation of conscious events that he has brought to pass in the sensibilities of other people plus the accumulation of conscious events which other people have brought to pass in him. James thus finds the central locus of life in the sensible consciousness, thereby discovering, too, that the search for a solution to the problem of personal identity has led him right back into the familiar surroundings of his major theme.

Chapter Eight

FALSE VALUES

SINCE THE BULK of James's fiction builds and adorns a new standard of values incompatible with the received standard in general use, the values which are conventionally held in high esteem are dishonored therein by implication rather than by direct impeachment. An occasional James story, however, makes a frontal assault on an accepted value. These stories, by manifest intention, undermine the respect which is usually exacted by, and the repute which is usually accorded to, the attainment of such objectives of desire and ambition as social position, fame, foreign travel, or any other advantage which enhances self-esteem by proclaiming one's superiority or elevation over one's fellowmen.

The earliest story in this genre draws a distinction between the pleasure of possessing a reputation for talent and the pleasure of possessing and exercising the talent itself, between the pretender who succeeds in securing the pleasure which the outward and displayed tokens of esteem can bestow and the true genius whose joy in his work depends but faintly on public recognition. The narrator, in *The Sweetheart Of M. Briseux* (1873), rescues herself from her impending marriage to Harold Staines, handsome and wealthy but not the painter he thinks he is, by permitting a threadbare but vehement young man, M. Briseux, who had entered Staines's studio unannounced, to finish the portrait of her which Staines had begun. Briseux's painting is a work of genius, and Harold is

131

so jealous that he breaks off the engagement. One hour in the presence of an authentic artist had broken for the girl, who never sees either one of them again, the spell cast by a pretentious imposter.

The next story in which James deflates invidious esteem for a reputed advantage satirizes the supposed, easily won, and frequently exploited endowments which accrue to the foreign traveler. Mrs. Susan Daintry, in *A New England Winter* (1884), greatly overestimates her son Florimond, whose mediocre qualities are hidden from the undiscerning by the romantic aura with which a long Parisian residence as a student painter had endowed him. To the amusement of Lucretia Daintry, Florimond's aunt, who sees through him, Rachel Torrance, the girl with whom Susan fears her son will fall in love, also detects the jejunity underneath Florimond's easy manners. When Susan finally discovers that Florimond is carrying on a flirtation with a light and foolish married woman, Mrs. Pauline Mesh, she hurries him back to Paris. James here satirizes the tendency of Americans to credulously overvalue the benefits of a European residence, which often permits a pretentious mediocrity to pass in America for an elegant and superior being.

The evils of nationalistic patriotism are emphatically stressed in two of James's shorter fictions. Agatha Grice, in *The Modern Warning* (1888), commits suicide because she cannot endure the hostility between two persons to each of whom she feels a personal loyalty. One is her husband and the other is her brother. Her husband is anti-American and her brother is anti-British, and between them they bring about the death of a girl who loves them both. This story is a plea for a more sympathetic mutual understanding between the two nations.

Felix Vendemer, in *Collaboration* (1892), runs afoul of nationalistic antipathies which sunder an association based on artistic sympathies. Felix, a French poet, forms an alliance with Herman, a German composer; because of the affinity between their approach to and treatment of their respective arts they decide to collaborate and compose an opera. Whereupon politics divides what art had joined together. Felix' French fiancée breaks her engagement to him because she hates Germans, Herman's brother cuts off his allowance because he hates Frenchmen, and their opera, however great as an artistic creation, will probably never find a producer.

Social position, the cause to which so many persons devote the major efforts of their lives and the enjoyment of which is so universally assumed to be without question a token of intrinsic merit, is subjected to basically caustic and ironical treatment in two stories by James. These disclosures of the devious and doubtful means by which social position can be acquired discredit the very theory of an élite. James goes far enough behind the façade of recognized social superiority to discern the unacknowledged but genuine disbelief of the elite in the grounds of their own pretentions and tacit claims.

Rose Tramore, in *The Chaperone* (1891), succeeds against great odds in re-establishing her mother in the good graces of the social group from which she had alienated herself by an act morally offensive to the conventions of the group.

The reason for which society re-admits Mrs. Tramore to the status of respectability by implication betrays the truly adventitious character of the nominal credentials supposedly exacted of persons enjoying social approval. The irony of the narrative develops from the implied but steadily emerging incongruity between the assumed and the real values subscribed to by the moral snob.

When Rose was but a child, her mother had absconded with a lover who had met sudden death before sufficient time had elapsed for divorce and remarriage. From that time until her grown daughter came to her rescue, Mrs. Tramore had been ostracized from society, although her private life had been impeccable but for her one lapse from virtue. Upon reaching maturity, and upon her father's death, Rose, who had been raised by her father's people, decides to move to her mother's house and share her mother's destiny. She refuses to visit anyone who does not invite her mother also. Rose is a charming girl and people want her, but Rose remains adamant in her resolve that to get her they must take her mother too. One shrewd hostess finally perceives the oddity and the social rarity of this reversal of the usual situation, the spectacle of the daughter who takes the mother out. A veritable debut party is arranged, and Charlotte Vesey, socially prominent, introduces to society the woman, Mrs. Tramore, who is chaperoned by her daughter Rose. The mother and daughter thereupon become the social feature at many a social gathering. Rose has succeeded, and before long her mother goes about alone, once again a member of society in good standing.

134

Mamie Cutter, in the story called *Mrs. Medwin* (1901), effects a breach in the excluding walls of polite society for the entry of the dowdy but moneyed Mrs. Medwin and thereby earns the fat fee which Mrs. Medwin had promised to pay her for the social service. Mamie's opportunity to secure for Mrs. Medwin an invitation to the house of Lady Wantridge comes when a chance encounter between Scott Homer, Mamie's disreputable but traveled and entertaining half brother, and Lady Wantridge results in the latter's desire for Homer's presence at a dinner party at which the principal guest is to be a Grand Duke whose jaded senses require some such odd character as Homer for stimulation. Mamie, however, will not let Mrs. Wantridge have Homer unless she takes Mrs. Medwin too—and this is what Lady Wantridge is finally forced to do.

Another respected value which James, like Ibsen, felt to be often if not usually mere face value with benefit of cosmetics is the maintenance of moral appearances. Arthur Prime, in *Paste* (1900), lies and disposes of evidence not rightfully his in order to avoid admitting that his stepmother had not always lived an upright moral life. To preserve appearances, Arthur violates the Puritan moral code in the interest of which the appearances were to be preserved. Among his stepmother's effects after her death was found a pearl necklace of great value, which could not have been given her by Arthur's father, who was a poor vicar, and which must therefore have been a present from some lover when she was an actress, prior to her marriage. Arthur gives all the stored mementos of his stepmother's stage life, including the pearls, to his cousin Charlotte, hoping that she will never discover their value. Charlotte makes the discovery, however, and brings the incriminating pearls back to him. Arthur angrily denies that they are anything but paste, promises to have them appraised, and subsequently informs Charlotte that they have proved to be worthless. She, however, afterwards sees a wealthy lady wearing the identical pearls and learns from her that they had been purchased for a huge sum. Arthur's puritanical moral principles had evidently eroded and warped his sense of truth.

The careful preservation of personal beauty normally wrings admiring and envious tribute from a compliant public, but James directs our attention to that deeper and undissembling beauty which, consonant with any age, presents a visible surface harmonious with the invisible character, the true self. Lady Nina Beldonald, in *The Beldonald Holbein* (1901), governs her life on the theory that emotionally deep living leaves marks on a face harmful to its beauty; she chooses to live a cautious, shallow, placid life in order to preserve her beauty. And it is for the purpose of accentuating her beauty that she takes with her wherever she goes a maid or paid companion, carefully selected for plainness of feature. Her selection of Louisa Brash, however, was a mistake that revealed the flaw in her theory. Nina saw in Louisa Brash only a plain-faced old woman, whose face was marred by the deep lines which a long and full life had placed there. However, the first time Louisa appears in public with her mistress, two prominent artists excitedly request permission to paint her. They tell Nina that Louisa has the face of a great

Holbein, that she possesses a "perfection of a little white old face in which every wrinkle was the touch of a master." Louisa soon becomes a celebrated beauty, much to Nina's bewilderment and discomfiture. In anger and exasperation, Lady Beldonald finally dismisses Louisa Brash and replaces her with a young and pretty maid, whose prettiness can be exhausted by one good look.

The last of the shallow values, prized by the nameless multitude as well as by the famous few, but more realistically and prudently appraised by James, is fame. The two stories which James wrote on this subject tenderly and patiently dissect the morphology of fame, and his thoughtful investigative surgery quietly dissipates the supposed magical properties of renown.

Morris Gedge, in *The Birthplace* (1903), becomes acquainted with the seamy side of fame by observing it from the close range of his position as custodian and guide to the house, now a national shrine, in which a great Poet had been born. Morris had been thrilled by his appointment to this post and had looked forward, before undertaking his duties, to a consecrate sense of communion with the spirit of the great Poet. But he soon learns that what the visiting tourists want is legendary detail of the Poet's private life, trivialities which fritter away the poetic associations of the Birthplace. Morris nearly loses his job before he disciplines his inclination to adhere to strict historical accuracy in his discourses to the tourists; he is compelled to enlarge on local legends, to invent probabilities that excite tourist interest. When Morris finally gives free rein to his fancy and deliberately falsifies history, when he becomes completely fraudulent as a commentator and guide, only then does he please his masters. But Morris mourns in secret, because he knows that the spirit of the great Poet no longer resides in the Birthplace, profaned as his fame is there.

Howard Bight and Maud Blandy, in *The Papers* (1903), abandon in disgust their means of livelihood: journalism consisting of the contribution to newspapers of items of publicity interest concerning persons desirous of public attention. Howard and Maud learn so much about how public fame is created, how little it correlates with intrinsic individual merit, how disintegrating its effect on those who possess it, and how debasing the desire for it on those who do not, that their stomachs are finally turned and they are impelled to change their occupation.

Howard had succeeded, by deft publicity, in making a Prominent Public Man of Beadel-Muffet, who was really a less than ordinary member of Parliament; while Maud had failed, being less apt at her work, in creating a public interest in Mortimer Marshall, who was a playwright of some merit. When Beadel-Muffet, who has basked for years in the publicity Howard has created for him, asks Howard to cease his activities in his behalf, pretending that a Mrs. Chorner, whom he wishes to marry, is so fastidious that she finds so-frequent mention of him in the public press offensive, Howard refuses to believe him. Whereupon Beadel-Muffet disappears, and it is mysteriously rumored that he has committed suicide. Maud introduces her protégé, Mortimer Marshall, to Howard; and when Howard, noticing how avid

Marshall is for personal publicity, facetiously but solemnly offers to center public attention on him by publishing a false report to the effect that Marshall has news of Beadel-Muffet's whereabouts, Marshall eagerly accepts the offer, unable to resist the low bribe. This disgusts both Maud and Howard. Maud is further disgusted when she interviews Mrs. Chorner with reference to Beadel-Muffet's disappearance and discovers that that lady's pretended fastidious disapprobation of mention in the public press is really a disguised desire for publicity of a more sensational character. Finally, both Maud and Howard are thoroughly revolted by Beadel-Muffet's reappearance and admission that the suicide rumors had been planted by himself as a hoax—for publicity's sake. These three variants of baseness—Mrs. Chorner's, Mortimer Marshall's, and Beadel-Muffet's—convince Howard and Maud that the very concept itself of public fame is debasing and that they cannot, in self-respect, have anything further to do with it.

———

These ten stories test the value of several commodities commonly held to be worth working for. James finds them wanting, not because to desire them means that we confound the token of a value with the value itself, but because they fail to do for us what an expanding consciousness does: enlarge the understanding. They merely flatter our conception of the appearance we present to the eyes of others. The authority of selfhood can only be buttressed by the external props of these false values, while a true value will add new strength and mastery to the inner and essential man.

Chapter Nine

THE INTERNATIONAL THEME

WILLIAM DEAN HOWELLS, a contemporary and lifelong champion of James's work and reputation, set the fashion of regarding the international theme as James's principal contribution to fiction. In doing so, Howells did James more harm than good. A more exacting and thorough examination of James's fiction in its totality, now that we have his completed work available to us and can review his earliest stories in the light of his latest, reveals that James's actual theme deals with much deeper realities than mere international differences.

To describe James's stories and novels as accounts of Americans in Europe is to describe them in terms of the counters he used in telling the stories instead of in terms of the essential meaning of the stories themselves. *Daisy Miller*, for instance, is not the story of an American girl in Rome and in conflict with the social taboos in force there but a study of any girl in any place reacting headily to public criticism based on misunderstanding of her behavior and to her lover's craven fear of public opinion and his reluctance to champion her. *The Ambassadors* is not a story of a provincial American receiving a Parisian education late in life but a study of any man at any time and in any place feeling his way through a delicate situation which is morally unfamiliar to him. *The Golden Bowl* does not tell of innocent

Americans in conflict with wicked Europeans but of any people in any time and place succeeding in mastering a lower emotion by means of a higher one.

The attempt to discover the meaning of James's fiction in the fact that many of his characters are Americans temporarily residing in Europe is fruitless. The incidental can seldom provide a clue to the essential. Americans in Europe and Europeans in relation to Americans in Europe happen to have been the particular classes of people with which James was acquainted; they became therefore the natural symbols, the adventitious particulars, by means of which he conveyed his meanings. Failure to abstract his true inward meanings from the means he used is, however, mere literalizing pedantry.

Each one of James's "international" novels has turned out, upon examination, to be only incidentally international and to be in fact a discourse on some other and deeper theme. Three short stories, however, address themselves directly and principally to the theme of international differences. They are: *A Bundle Of Letters*, *The Point Of View*, and *Miss Gunton Of Poughkeepsie*.

Miranda Hope, in *A Bundle Of Letters* (1879), spends some weeks in a Parisian boarding house with fellow guests consisting of a girl from New York City, a young man from Boston, an English girl, a Frenchman, and a German. Miranda herself is a Maine girl. Self-revealing letters from the six people to their friends contain comments on the other five. The least provincial and most comprehensive point of view, although slightly priggish, is Miranda's. The one characteristic shared by the other five—but not by Miranda —is a sense of pleasure in excluding certain other classes of people from the kind of personal expansion each is enjoying. James here isolates the one New World personal attribute of which he most approves.

Marcellus Cockerel, in *The Point Of View* (1882), presents his impression of the American way of life in contrast to the European. He is a young American attorney who has just returned from a year's tour of Europe. His impressions are compared with those of an American girl who has lived in Europe since the age of eight, of her mother who has lived in Europe for fifteen years, of an American woman of fifty-eight who divides her residence between Europe and America, of a young Bostonian who spends his summers in Paris, and of two Europeans traveling in America, one a member of the British Parliament and the other of the French Academy. The only one who understands what he sees is Cockerel, and he is most vehement in his approval of the American scene. He is the only one who is aware of the tremendous social drama being enacted in the United States, a drama which is giving birth to a new kind of man: one who recognizes only horizontal, not vertical, class distinctions. James here declares his preference for a world in which social classes exist side by side rather than superimposed one on the other.

Lily Gunton, in *Miss Gunton Of Poughkeepsie* (1900), repudiates her engagement to marry a Roman prince because his mother refuses to obey the American custom of making the first advance to the son's prospective bride in the form of a written invitation to call. The Princess insists that Miss Gunton obey the Roman custom, which prescribes that the prospective daughter-in-law be the one to take the initial step. Yielding to her son's entreaties, the Princess finally accedes to the American custom, but she has waited too long. Lily has broken off the engagement and formed a new one with an American named Adam P. Bransby. So the love between the American girl and the Roman boy does not come to fruition in marriage because the American girl can see that the European custom of making the husband's family clan the social unit results in the absorption of the girl into the depths of the husband's family, while the American way of making each married couple the social unit enables the girl to retain more of her individuality as a person. The seemingly trivial question as to who is to write the first letter, the bride or the mother-in-law, becomes a symbol, a focal point, of the clash between two great traditions with respect to the place and function of love and marriage in the social order.

————

These three stories express James's acceptance of, and matured agreement with, his American heritage. He marks off and defines wherein the New World temper differs from the Old, and he not only affirms but elucidates the reasons for his sympathy with the American point of view and his dissent from the European. He definitely ranges himself on the side of those who hold that the individual citizen of a commonwealth benefits by the destruction rather than by the erection and maintenance of social barriers such as caste divisions, group exclusiveness, and family-clan rather than husband-wife nuclear relationships. The common denominator of the three positions attacked in these three stories is the European assumption that the exclusion of other human beings from the group to which one belongs automatically confers an excellence on those within the excluding barriers. James contends, on the other hand, that those barriers deny exit from, as well as entrance to, the enclosed areas and in so doing deprive the protected ones of access to experience necessary to their growth.

James stated the characteristic difference between American and European social customs in this way: that the American tended to dilate man's experience of the world and the European to constrict it. James's deep and innate predilection in favor of an expanding consciousness left him no choice but to defend, honor, and extol the New World answer to this ancient issue.

Chapter Ten

FABLES FOR CRITICS

O N THE SUBJECT of the creative artist, his work and
his relation to society, James wrote nine stories. Artists
and writers were used by James as characters in many other
stories, but only in these nine does their craft have essential
bearing on the actual theme of the fiction.

James regarded man as primarily a creator, and his activities intrinsically and internally and truly satisfying to him
only insofar as they gratify the demands of his creative
urge. Man is so constituted that only through some kind of
creative activity can expansion of consciousness take place.
Some degree of creativity subsists in every kind of human
action, but the purest form of creativity manifests itself in
the creative artist. He does completely what other people
do only partially. He abstracts from human behavior the
one aspect which makes it valuable to man and endeavors
to make that aspect coextensive with the totality of his own
action in life.

This Jamesian conception of man as creator, and of the
artist as man wholly devoted to creative work, sets the highest value on the men of his craft. And in these nine stories of
creative artists he became their spokesman. In their name he
accepted and defined the responsibilities of the artist, and
for them he bespoke the deserts due them. He wrote stories

to guide the artist out of the enchanted bog of nonproductive absorption in past art, to warn both artist and public that art is more than a mere transcription of life, to direct the public's attention to the art works created by the artist and away from the artist as man, and to uproot the critics' habit of speculation on the possible effects which a different personal life would have had on an artist's work—a habit which James exposes as a maneuver by which critics avoid direct examination of an artist's actual achievement. These nine stories, commentaries as they are on the ways in which the public uses its artists, form a primer of elementary principles, the application of which would enable the public to gain what the artist has to give.

Mr. Theobald, in *The Madonna Of The Future* (1873), prepares and plans for so long a time to paint the picture which is to be his life's masterpiece and to make love to the woman who is to be its subject that he dies of old age before making the first overt move towards accomplishing the joint project. By procrastination he makes of his life a monument to sexual and artistic impotence. Theobald is a great talker and an untiring student of painted Madonnas, but the drug of past art and of his own eloquence paralyzes his creative will for so long that he loses the power to perform any act of life except that of adoration vocally expressed. This power he does have, and this story commemorates it, but his tragic last days make clear to Theobald that the enjoyment of created art is no substitute for creative work.

Major and Mrs. Monarch, in *The Real Thing* (1893), fail as models for illustrations to a society novel, in spite of the fact that, having been in society all their lives, they are the real thing and not merely professional models dressed up to look like society people. The artist who employs them is compelled to give them up and return to the use of his Italian valet and a "freckled cockney" by the name of Miss Churm. The real thing in life proves not to be the real thing in art, which is James's pertinent commentary on photographic naturalism and reportorial art: it is so much less realistic than is representational art.

The narrator, in *The Aspern Papers* (1888), attempts to purloin some love letters written long ago by Jeffrey Aspern (Shelley) to, and in the present possession of, his now aged mistress, Juliana Bordereau (Jane Clairmont). She foils him, however, asserting her exclusive private right to the mementos of the intimate life of the great poet and denying any public right to them. The story tells of a deep duel between a modern democratic violator of the private lives of famous folk and a late-surviving representative of the traditional aristocratic thesis that constituted privacy is a defensible and an inalienable luxury—and the winner of the duel is the aged lady.

The narrator, in *John Delavoy* (1898), refuses to comply with a magazine editor's peremptory request that he revise the article he had written about the illustrious and recently deceased author, John Delavoy. The editor wants less interpretive analysis of Delavoy's themes and more gossipy commentary on the famous author's private life. Delavoy's daughter, who is being wooed by both men, chooses to marry the author of the article and to dismiss the editor, indicating

147

thereby her conviction that a truer service is done for her father, whom she adores, by him who interprets his creative work for the few than by him who promotes his personal fame among the many.

George Withermore, in *The Real Right Thing* (1900), abandons his attempt to write the memoirs of Ashton Doyne, the distinguished writer recently deceased. A series of events convinces him that the really right thing to do on an artist's behalf is to direct attention to his published work rather than to the personal details of his private history. Mrs. Ashton Doyne had invited George to write a biography of Ashton, and she had placed at his disposal Ashton's private study and all the personal papers it contained. Strange things soon begin to happen: papers disappear, letters lose themselves, sorted materials suddenly and unaccountably become disarranged. George begins to sense the presence of Ashton's ghost. Mrs. Doyne also has a queer feeling that Ashton is in the house. Then one evening George finds Ashton Doyne standing, as plain as in life, in the doorway to the study, barring entrance. George finally reads the meaning of this symbolic barrier: that to publish biographical detail about an artist's life is injurious to the identity presented to the world by the artist himself in his own work.

Dencombe, in *The Middle Years* (1893), becomes at least partially reconciled to his approaching early death by finding that at least one reader of the books he has written passionately admires them. Dencombe is dying before he has finished his work, before he has adequately and completely transferred himself to paper. He bitterly resents this trick of fate, until he learns that his doctor is so ardent an admirer of his books that he forsakes another patient—and a tremendous fee—to minister to the last days of his favorite author, Dencombe. This proof that he has made somebody care assures Dencombe that a measure of real achievement has been vouchsafed him. His need for and response to this token is James's admonition to the public that its responsibility as an audience cannot be slighted without injuring the creative artist.

Ralph Limbert, in *The Next Time* (1895), writes novel after novel, attempting each time to produce a potboiler but finding instead that he has another masterpiece on his hands. Each next attempt to produce a potboiler creates another "deep and delicate thing," another "unscrupulous, unsparing, shameless, merciless masterpiece," "charming with all his charm and powerful with all his power." His readers and sales dwindle in number with each novel he publishes and he has to write continually faster in order to support his family. His books improve in quality while his income shrinks, and he finally dies of overwork. This amusing story is James's revenge on his own public, which had begun to desert him in the nineties.

Hugh Vereker, in *The Figure In The Carpet* (1896), complains that the critics of his books write only twaddle about him, that they completely miss the inner meaning and intention of his work. A young critic by the name of Corvick finds this complaint so challenging that he devotes six months to a close study of the text of Vereker's work. He finds the figure in the carpet of Vereker's text, its inner meaning and intention, but it takes six months' hard labor to do it. This story is essentially an open letter to literary critics, admonishing them to pay closer attention to the creative works they examine, to pay them the courtesy of a more analytic appreciation. The story voices James's protest against inadequate, cursory examination of his productions and his request that his work be treated with more awareness of its full content.

Spencer Brydon, in *The Jolly Corner* (1908), meets face to face the ghost of the man he would have been had he spent the previous twenty-three years of his life in America instead of in Europe. He had arrived back in America only a few weeks ago, at the age of fifty-six, and has already formed the habit of wandering at night time through the empty, ancestral house in which he would have lived had he stayed in America. He begins to sense a presence there, and stalks it, feeling sure that it is the wraith of the self he had abandoned when he went to live abroad. The wraith had possessed sufficient vital force to go right on living without him.

When the other Spencer Brydon eventually shows himself, the real Spencer recoils in horror: the face is indubitably his face, but it is also the face of a black stranger. Spencer falls to the floor in unconscious stupor. When he awakens the ghost is gone, and with it has vanished Spencer's curiosity as to what qualitative difference in his personal identity might have resulted from a choice on his part of some other environment and way of life. By grappling with this query, and, by exploring, mastering it, Spencer discovers that one must inevitably feel any possible alternate personal identity, should one see it closely enough, to be foreign and hateful, as evil as an imposter's caricature of one's real self.

———————

At the bottom of all these stories, except the first two, lies James's exasperation with the tendency among critics to interpret a work of art in some other terms than those implanted in the work of art itself. This, of course, has been the vice of modern criticism. It is stronger today than it was in James's own lifetime and, in spite of James's censure, it is even now the prevailing vice of many critics who write about James himself.

An arrogant disregard of the purport of his fiction, a refusal to assess the weight of his themes or his success or failure to fully set them forth, a neglect to even informatively state them, has notably characterized the bulk of the critical writing on James's work. This sabotage of them eanings he placed in his fiction has taken the form of the very critical method (or bankruptcy of method) which he excoriated in half a dozen or more works of fiction. The futility of attempting to interpret a work of art in the light of the artist's private life and the consequent injustice to the artist's created work—the very phenomenon to which James had called our attention and cautioned us against as early as 1888—were promptly manifested (and the truth of his contention unintentionally and inadvertently demonstrated) by the critics of James's own work. Even to this day James's novels are too frequently construed, not in terms of what they actually have to say for themselves, but in the light only of the fact of James's European residence and other even more minor facts or speculations about his private life.

However, the meanings which James placed in his novels are still there and James himself has shown us the way to master them. The formula is simplicity itself—simply a request to read, attentively and reflectively, the text of his fiction. His art was his life, the milestones in his life were the books he published; and if we want to know what manner of man he was, there is no better source for that knowledge than the masterpieces of fiction he left us. To discover what they say, by reading them, is to learn to know the man.

CONCLUSION

THE UNIQUENESS OF JAMES, the single new thought in the world to which his fiction gives expression, consists in his recognition that sensitivity to other persons expands the consciousness. James's greatness as man and artist, all the edifices of his thought and the very texture of his sentences, grew from the fertile soil of this idea. It not only impregnates the thought content of his themes but also directs the turn of phrase and gives strength and grace and movement to his prose rhythms. The man and his art are so completely identified with the idea that they seem to be three incarnations of one essence.

James's work does not intellectually or philosophically expound the idea; it embodies the idea in an art form. The characters in his novels do not even discuss the idea or elucidate it in any way except by their characteristic action. It is so implicit in their nature that only an outside observer can make the abstraction and define their personal timbre.

The thematic synthesis which is here presented as the purport—the figure in the carpet—of James's fiction is derived from and built upon an analytic inspection of the TEXT of James's fiction. The idea is discoverable in the fiction itself and is the natural product of an inspection, free from preconceived notions, of the entire range of James's writings. With the completion of James's final work in fiction, the idea stands revealed as the Jamesian canon, the law by which he tests not only the individual nature but entire civilizations.

This pivotal center of James's thought—that the quality of one's sensitivity to other persons determines the growth of one's greatest possession, consciousness—radiates a conditioning influence on all other aspects of his world view. By locating the source of value in the relations man conducts with his fellow men, rather than in economic goods or in supernatural considerations or in scientific knowledge, it stamps him as a humanist; by resolutely confining his attention and the scope of his study to the contemporary grain of the world's human product, man, rather than to his economic, supernatural, or scientific history and destiny, it identifies him as an artist; and by asserting the universal applicability, not only to the artist but to all mankind, of the principle that growth of consciousness is the foremost boon in life, it supplies him with the essential elements of a world view.

The pressure, never weak and never violent, of a James sentence on the mind of a reader is similar in character to the kind of pressure which, in a Jamesian world, would hold between people. That resilience which is the dominant quality of a James sentence, that scrupulous renouncing of shock and sudden assault while at the same time remitting no jot of its demand on a reader's attentiveness and intelligence, illustrates the attribute which James would require of all human intercourse. For the want of that attribute, much of the life which James observed in the world about him—and which he then imaginatively reproduced in his fiction—fell for him into patterns of emotional cannibalism: arrogant moral opinion, meddling, parasitism, coercion, exploitation, revenge.

154

These modes of behavior correspond to flaws in the personal grain of representative human beings, persons qualitatively representative of the human race during James's historical period. James's apprehension of the world was neither intellectual nor philosophic nor scientific but aesthetic, in the sense that the main object of his examination was to determine an individual's fineness or coarseness of texture. James did not deal in causes or in historical analysis; he dealt with the end product only—which is man as he is today. And this man—the composite man of his time—James found unsatisfactory, for definite reasons fully elaborated in his fiction.

I

James's fiction, taken in its entirety, diagnoses a sickness, and a sickness not only of one country or of one class, but of a civilization. James noticed that sickness primarily as it manifests itself in personal relations, but it flourishes not only there but in all other departments of modern life as well. It is the major sickness of an era in human history, an era which began as far back as the thirteenth century, when the medieval synthesis began to break up.

The decline of the concept of the soul has been accompanied by a corresponding decline in the ability of human beings to respect one another. Mankind—at least Western man—has not yet relearned the art of mutual respect which was lost when supernatural grounds for it disintegrated. That natural grounds exist on which it can be rebuilt is the conspicuous fact to which James's fiction attests.

The specific indictment which James brought against an aspect of the practice of personal relations—the misemployment of human beings by one another—is also a general indictment against the civilization of modern times. People misuse one another not only in personal and social relations but also in the economic, political, international, and racial relations subsisting between the organized groups which make up civilized society; and the kind of misuse which James discovered and dissected in the field of personal relations is identical with the kind which iniquitously flourishes in these more public fields.

We have only to name such phenomena as economic imperialism, unlimited national sovereignty, national isolationism, trade barriers, the familiar economic and cultural treatment of subject and backward races, the treatment of Negroes in America, racial superiority complexes, the economy of scarcity, the exploitation of class by class, in order to perceive instantaneously the bearing which any application of James's central idea would have on these phenomena. They are the public counterparts of the sickness which James isolated in private lives. The fiber of the composite man is reproduced in the public aspects of the civilization which has prevailed in the Western world throughout some recent centuries. The two World Wars of the twentieth century corroborated James's diagnosis of the ills of modern man and modern times: the wars were the logical end and upshot of the sick world which James saw and described.

New ideas are coming alive in the world today, however, which may transform Western civilization and make it more congruous with the kind of world that James wanted. The growing recognition, for instance, that we cannot indefinitely maintain our material standard of living in America unless we aid the peoples of other and foreign areas of the earth's surface to bring their standard up to our level; that mere confiscation of the natural wealth of a backward or subject people does not contribute to the wealth of a predatory nation nearly so much as does a fostering of the native utilization of those resources, since the latter develops exchange markets for economic goods while the former does not; that economic and political and cultural isolationism (the concept of the sheltered life in another sphere) stunts the life of the national as well as that of the personal organism; that the national and world economy can be planned for productive abundance instead of being permitted to remain by default in the hands of a minority that battens on chaos and scarcity—the growing currency of ideas such as these may result in a major structural change not only in world civilization but also in the standard of values and personal grain of the composite man of our time.

The central ideas in James's fiction regarding the world of man's personal relations with his fellow men were forerunners of, and perhaps to some extent the ancestors of, ideas such as these in the world of economic and political, national and international, group relations. Who knows to what extent the internationalism with which James's name has always been associated and the tenor of James's criticism of our personal usage of one another have actually engendered ideas of this type in our economic and political thinking?

The influence of a major creative artist, as it seeps down through the writings of lesser artists who have been influenced by him and are more widely read by the general public, is incalculable in its range.

The significant fact that both isolationism and imperialism are losing prestige as modes of behavior among nations and that both these modes of behavior in private lives were the principal objects of attack in James's fiction renders the work of Henry James singularly apropos to the *zeitgeist* of our time. As the emotional cannibalism in personal behavior, such as we see in *The Turn Of The Screw*, gave way in James's fiction to the emotionally enlightened and less self-destructive conduct in *The Golden Bowl*, so the belligerent and exploitive character of Western civilization, in both its economic-and-political and national-and-international phases, is giving way to a new order of ideas more consonant with the needs and capacities of mankind.

II

How, then, shall we evaluate the work of Henry James, the one hundred and twenty-five novels, novelettes, and short stories which embody his look at life? Is the idea which was primarily his subject useful to us? Is it true? Does acceptance of it and realization of its full import and implication necessitate any adjustment in our present system of ideas and effect any change in our behavior? Does it add interest and meaning and intention to our lives—or can we merely agree that it seems generally true and go on our way satisfied that none of our notions or habitual patterns of behavior need be disturbed? Shall the work of Henry James be absorbed into our literature and culture, into the body of accumulated intellectual and artistic tradition that we will pass on to future generations with the imprimatur of our time? Do we want to adopt the controlling idea, which the fictional actions he set before us were designed to signify, into our familiar set of general ideas? Is James's integral view of life a leaven which can with profit be assimilated by, and incorporated into the substance and organic tissue of, the composite mind of our time?

In answering these questions, we must first guard against conceiving of James's idea in terms of a moral maxim. A morality can be derived from James's idea of the nature of consciousness and how it operates, but the idea itself aims at being a total view of life rather than a morality or a system of manners. Although the practical effect of James's idea may be an advocacy of a theory of conduct, more consciousness rather than more goodness is the objective towards which effort is directed. A total view of life includes an ethic but the ethic itself constitutes only a small part of the total view.

The observation of life for an artistic purpose differs only in the degree of inclusiveness from its observation for an ethical, political, or intellectual purpose. The artistic purpose, when attained, embodies a sense of the whole in a created work of art, from which may then be extracted by analysis the ethical, political, intellectual, or other aspects of the life presented. The fiction of James gives us life sensuously lived, holding in solution the subordinate meanings which may be intellectually apprehended. James's novels express an idea, but they do not belong to the "novel of ideas" genre as do the works of H. G. Wells, Aldous Huxley, or D. H. Lawrence. The ideas in the novels of these three writers are held in imperfect solution, in that abstract statements of them, quasi-philosophic disquisitions, appear in the novels themselves, while in a James novel the ideas appear only in the guise of a symbolic action. The ideas have been fully digested by the imagination and have become human life in the mind of James before the actual writing of the novel. A fusion has taken place between the idea and the act, the idea has disappeared into the action—where it belongs in a mature work of art.

Another thing to keep in mind in judging the present and lasting truth and usefulness of James's central idea is that James was not, in any sense of the word, an intellectual. He did not set out to be, and his writings do not make an attempt at being, those of a philosophic historian or a systematic psychologist or an ethical theorizer. His central idea did not result from reflection on the historical or ideational causes for the current condition of the composite mind or from any moralistic thinking on the therapeutics of conduct. The idea which informs the spirit of his fiction represents his sensuous or aesthetic (the root meaning of "sensuous") response to the spectacle of personal intercourse. He simply gave as careful, acute, and resolute an account of human beings as he was able to contrive, and it remains for us to make as explicit a formulation as we can of the distilled sense contained therein.

James's central idea itself—that a scrupulous and attentive consideration for (and of) the feelings of others, an actively sensitive, sympathetic searching out of those feelings, creates an enlargement of consciousness in both the considerate person and the recipient of his consideration (the reverse of this conduct producing an opposite result) and that this enlargement of consciousness constitutes any man's most valuable acquisition in life—what can we say for this idea? Is it true that successive levels or stages of consciousness can be attained, with practice, by a voluntary use and application of this postulate of conduct? Is this postulate merely another moral precept, destined to go the way of all the other ineffectual and fruitless moral precepts with which man has been plagued, or has James really hit upon an exact statement, description, and explanation of a basic, factual, continuing event in human behavior?—a statement that clarifies with a flash of illumination obscurely understood processes ceaselessly going on in the human world of which we are a part?

III

The claim that James makes for his conception of the behavior of consciousness is simply that those people who have once travèled from a lower to a higher level of awareness do actually understand how they got there, and that, moreover, they never return. This claim, I think, is not open to controversy. Introspection verifies it and by universal consent we know it to be a fact of experience.

Every one knows, from parallels in his own life, that those feelings of emotional admiration which Mrs. Newsome and the American Adelaide Wenham had once evoked from Lambert Strether and Frank Granger will be evoked no more, that acquaintance with Marie de Vionnet and the English Adelaide has changed the two men and taught them to see the true inferiority of what they had, in their previous unenlightened state, thought admirable. And every one, in casting his mind back over his own personal history, associates every essential step in the growth of his mind with an act of attention to some other person. People appear in one another's consciousnesses as meanings—symbols of a point of view; and the wiser we are the more aware we are of how much others had to do with every accession of wisdom, however small, which has come to us. Fresh meanings chemically combining, as it were, with ours create emergent new meanings in our minds. Inability to use other people in this way signifies a stasis in the development of one's mental structure (Waymarsh, in *The Ambassadors*), and the violent imposition of one's meanings on other people (emotional cannibalism) ushers in a regressive deterioration of intellect.

The claim that can now, in this third decade after James's death, be made for James's conception is that in the civil war in which Western civilization has been engaged, the challenging precipitator of the conflict crystallized in a national mobilization that very power neurosis against which, as manifested in private personal living, James directed the full weight of his art. Belief in the desirability of power over others—the core of nazi-fascist ideology—has existed and grown side by side in recent centuries with the contradictory belief in the desirability of individual freedom. Nineteenth-century political liberalism, attempting to negotiate between and reconcile these opposites (the democratic formula and exploitive, imperialist practice), innocently played into the hands of the power addicts. The nazi-fascist apotheosis of the power idea deifies one strand in our tradition and destroys all the others—or, in James's field of discourse, exalts over all others one fiber, the precise one that James disliked and excoriated, in the personal grain of the composite man of his time.

The extraordinary relevance of James's creative outlook to the specific social and political problem which will be taxing the keenest minds of our race during the balance of this century—the problem of how to be free though organized, how to plan our economic life without destroying our personal liberties—needs only be noticed to be recognized. How to introduce order into our economic chaos without ordering people around with coercive and bureaucratic arbitrariness will require an understanding of man's psychological wants as well as of his economic needs. The blight that could descend upon the expanding consciousness from a too executive and authoritarian, close-fitting and tightly organized social economy, the blight that would result from an increase instead of a diminution of interference by one man in the life of another has been envisioned as one of the chief dangers immediately confronting us. The evils of power may reappear in new forms in the society of the future unless the counteracting potency in the ideas of such men as Henry James gets freer play in our future intellectual culture than it has in the past.

IV

The final estimate of the creative work of Henry James—
or of any other artist—must necessarily depend, however,
not on its instrumental value in ethical, political, or intellectual bearings, but on its strictly artistic and imaginative
energy. The ability to excite the imagination into activity
provides fiction at its best with its peculiar functional
superiority over informational dissertations, and the degree
to which James's fiction possesses this power determines the
intrinsic merit of his work.

The pertinent question to ask and answer in testing the
quality of James's fiction (or of any fiction and of any art
form)—does it expand the consciousness?—refers us back to
James's own thesis regarding the way in which expansion of
consciousness comes about. We discover that the theme of
James's fiction contains not only an account of the nature of
consciousness and a statement of the effects of personal relations on consciousness: it also contains an aesthetic, an interpretation of the artistic process itself. A work of art expands
the consciousness, then, in the degree to which it reveals an
attentive, considerate, and sympathetic awareness of the
feelings of others on the part of the artist. And the reader
of a novel finds his consciousness expanding in the same
way as it does in his personal relations: by temporarily
abandoning his own identity, feelings, and attitudes, and
by experimentally borrowing, one after the other, those
of the characters in the novel. Thus does James make
interchangeable the criteria of human and of aesthetic
evaluation.

An experimental submission to the work of Henry James will excite a reader's imagination by inuring it primarily to conceive of individuals not as intelligent or unintelligent, moral or immoral, rich or poor, white or black, religious or irreligious, high-caste or low-caste, polite or impolite, male or female, but as fine-grained or coarse-grained. James's fiction is so imbued with this insight into the paramount jurisdiction of personal timbre that, after it has once swept through his imagination, the reader will discern its presence in every fragment of James's fiction. And never again will he quite be able to see people with the same eyes as those he had seen them with before the Jamesian way of seeing them had been impressed upon him.

He may also find that James always takes for granted that the term "sensitive" connotes strength, not weakness, just as fine-grained timber is generally stronger than coarse-grained; that to be fine-grained means to be many-fibered, and so to possess more units over which to distribute the taken strain, thus dissipating it; and that to be "sensitive" means not to be easily hurt, but to possess sensing powers denied to the dull, to hold and use antennae which transmit to the sensitive man more news of life, as it were, than the coarser-grained people get. These assumptions beneath the surface of James's fiction become apparent to a reader only after he has read enough James to notice the constant use of the personal-timbre comparison between characters, the distinction by grain instead of by the more familiar categories.

A legitimate and possibly adverse criticism of James's total view is that his favorite method of measuring people proves in fact to be a dividing device rather than a unifying one. James defines and commemorates superiority rather than humanity; his search is not for the human core common to Everyman but for the distinction between the excellent and the base. His is a selective and discriminating outlook on the human scene, not a hearty acceptance of its totality. Reading James does not instill in us a feeling of kinship with all other human beings, as does the reading of Shakespeare, for instance. James is more likely, on the other hand, to leave in us a sense of removal from, and a diminution of tolerance for, certain people whom we would heretofore have been inclined to accept uncritically.

This fact, however, does not make James "precious," as opposed to "universal." James's view is a total view, applicable to all men and acceptable by all men, and it is therefore universal, not precious. Its patrician aspect follows from the preference by inferior people for inferior values, such as power over others and wealth greater than another's; it does not depend on the continuation and maintenance of an oppressed and inferior class. An augmented consciousness cannot be conceived of as a special privilege supported by the suppression of consciousness in others. A cardinal point in James is that one's own consciousness grows by nurturing the consciousness of others; one's tolerance diminishes only for those with whom some degree of reciprocation is impossible and for those emotional cannibals who attempt to invade and suppress us. Our care then must be to guard against our own impulse towards a retaliatory and counteroffensive act, because such action expends a portion of our own precious fund of consciousness.

A curious similarity and perhaps kinship exists between this Jamesian working principle and the practice of non-violent resistance by the peoples of the Orient. James never visited the Far East, nor did he ever disclose in his published writings any knowledge of, or interest in, Eastern thought. Perhaps he nevertheless inadvertently succeeded in doing what Kipling despaired of, regarding the East and West: inducing the twain to meet.

Another legitimate adverse criticism of James's total view is that it does not clearly demarcate, and thus guard against our confusing, two kinds of differentiation between characters: (a) by the subdegrees of their state of civilization, and (b) by the modes of their sensibility. James has a tendency to account for the latter in terms of the former and he often seems to assume that the situation he is presenting in a novel is an (a) situation when it is really (b). He disguises this oversimplification of character by his constant effort to present completely and without prejudice his unsympathetic characters, to state their case as well or better than they could have stated it themselves, but it remains as a definite limitation in his fiction. Mrs. Gereth's tragedy is a mitigated one, because, as James presents her, she is not a sufficient foil for, equal and opposite to, Fleda. Had James been able to envision Mrs. Gereth's mode of sensibility as equal to but different from Fleda's instead of as a lower degree of sensibility than Fleda's, *The Spoils Of Poynton* would have cut deeper into the issue. Had Lord Theign, in *The Outcry*, been a little less anachronistic, he could have stood for the timeless Tory mode of sensibility. Rose Armiger, in *The Other House*, although intellectually abler than any other character in the novel, disappoints us because James presents her as being merely deficient in civilization rather than as being victimized by her mode of sensibility. Notwithstanding a supreme effort of James's art to endow Kate Croy (*The Wings Of The Dove*) with a mode of sensibility able to stand alone, self-justified, we are not sure that she is anything better than a common little swindler.

Only in *The Golden Bowl* do we find a clear clash of sensibility between two equally civilized persons. Maggie and Amerigo equal each other in fineness of fibre, in personal timbre, and in degree of civilization, but possess irreconcilable modes of sensibility. Their marriage, which survived one of the worst catastrophes which could happen in a marriage, will never die, because their conflict of sensibility will never be resolved. Maggie and Amerigo will be eternally interested in each other because neither one can finally pass judgment on the other.

Since James so nearly overcame in the rest of his fiction the limitation that he completely transcended in *The Golden Bowl*, he must himself have been as conscious of the difficulty as we. The fact that in reading James we become continually aware of the distinction between a personal conflict due to variation in degree of enlightenment, one due to variation in personal fineness of grain, and one due to differences in mode of sensibility, indicates the presence of a struggle in James himself to differentiate between these types of conflict. His failure to master this distinction mars his account of personal relations by causing him to omit treatment of certain fundamental disparities which, since we know them to exist, we would like to see appear in James's fictional world. Persistently opposed ways of seeing the world, no one of them superior in any way to any other, we seldom find in a James narrative.

If James were not so passionately serious, if his own unique way of seeing the world were not so ingrained, his work would be romantic melodrama instead of humanistic art. His villains were not drawn from stock; he found his own villains and he profoundly hated and profoundly loved what his characters stood for. A cold and impersonal artist only in his methods, techniques, and execution, he was a man of deep feeling in the uses of his art. In fact, the one respect in which his fiction falls short of the greatest is directly due to his emotional participation in what he considered to be the worst kind of human suffering. He took sides on issues which to him were the most deep-reaching of his era and he was therefore advocate as well as artist. Had he been less advocate and more artist, he might have given us more modes of sensibility and less gradations in states of civilization.

V

This book, too, has been written from the point of view of an advocate as well as that of a critic. The critical method employed, however, has been that of attempting an account of (not commentary on) the contents and sense of James's fiction as accurate as James's fictional account of the world he saw. James did not distort human character to make his fiction represent his idea, and I have not distorted the meanings of James's fiction in order to advocate any idea of my own.

I advocate the reading of James, not only because I believe his idea to be true and important and an encounter with his mode of sensibility to be in itself a prepotent imaginative stimulus, but also because the sound and movement of his sentences—aside from their prose sense—are fully consonant with his meanings. James succeeded in achieving what all artists attempt: complete transference of the self to an external medium. The qualities of his mind, the characteristic physical motion of his body, the kind of ideas he espoused, the flavor of his personality—all are reproduced in the carriage and demeanor of his language. The timbre and tonality of the man are more intimately and utterly displayed by the powerful and graceful motion of his language than they could be by his physical presence. The lineaments of his prose are as individually and uniquely his own as are the lineaments of his face. We are as astonished at what a page of James's later, and especially his latest, writing does with language, with our old familiar words, as at what a new composer for piano, such as Prokofiev, does with the old and familiar twelve tones of the musical scale. James gained such mastery of his medium that his use of language is as unlike any one else's, either before or after him, as one man's face is unlike another's. His peculiar fragrance, inimitable and rare, emanates from his idea, so that we sense his meaning as much from the contour of his language as from the content.

The essential aim of the artistic and creative process—is it not simply to recreate in some external medium an exact counterpart of the creative artist's inner self? And does not religion itself maintain its hold on the imagination of the people because of the concept of God as creator rather than because of its promise of immortality? The enigmatic mystery of the creative act fascinates the human mind more profoundly and universally than any other phenomenon, and God as artist of the universe which manifests his attributes is the mythic archetype of the writer, painter, sculptor, architect, or whatever successfully externalizes his personal attributes in an art form. That is why we feel, however uncomfortably, that to be a ballet dancer is a greater thing than to be a senator.

James stands, then, in our literature as the exponent as well as the advocate of the expanded consciousness. His fiction testifies to his earned possession of the value which he prefers above all others and certifies for our preference too. The characters in some Jamesian scenes communicate to us so articulate and intense a sense of their individual and separate awarenesses—moving on swiftly in time—that we begin to know in a new way how it feels to be alive. The unspoken and unwritten thoughts between the lines of a characteristic Jamesian page outnumber the ones actually printed there. The tenor of each remark indicates that certain thoughts had occurred, sometimes to the character and sometimes to the author, between that remark and the one previous to it. These thoughts, although unspoken and unwritten, must nevertheless be retrieved and lived through by the reader if he is to get the full meaning of the printed words. This kind of writing makes such great demands on a reader's attention that it in reality amounts to a new mode of sensibility. The sheer measureable quantity of charged consciousness, of conscious mental life, in his fiction challenges the intellectual capacity and persistence of readers who are habituated to more conventional writing.

The reward which accrues to a reader who accepts and undergoes the Jamesian discipline is, however, immediate. The very next conversation he overhears or engages in will be more alive for him with unspoken meanings, because he will be awake to the thinking which is going on in the minds and between the remarks of the discoursers. Such unspoken thinking constantly occurs, even in the mind of a six-year-old child, but seldom do we consider—or are we even conscious of—anything but the audible spoken words. In consequence, we but partially understand the meaning of the words we hear. By putting us in possession of this inaudible conscious world, James makes a luminous addition to our powers of awareness. To have been able to convey mental life to such a charged degree, he himself must have been a completely conscious man.

THE END

INDEX OF STORIES

INDEX OF CHARACTERS

INDEX OF CHARACTERS

177